Do I look skinny in this house?

Do I look skinny in this house?

How to feel great in your home using Design Psychology

Kelli Ellis

NEW YORK

Do I look skinny in this house?
How to feel great in your home using Design Psychology

© 2014 Kelli Ellis.

Published in New York, New York, by Morgan James Publishing. Morgan James and The Entrepreneurial Publisher are trademarks of Morgan James, LLC. www.MorganJamesPublishing.com

The Morgan James Speakers Group can bring authors to your live event. For more information or to book an event visit The Morgan James Speakers Group at www.TheMorganJamesSpeakersGroup.com.

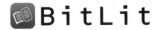
A FREE eBook edition is available
with the purchase of this print book

CLEARLY PRINT YOUR NAME IN THE BOX ABOVE

Instructions to claim your free eBook edition:
1. Download the BitLit app for Android or iOS
2. Write your name in UPPER CASE in the box
3. Use the BitLit app to submit a photo
4. Download your eBook to any device

ISBN 978-1-61448-897-2 paperback
ISBN 978-1-61448-898-9 eBook
ISBN 978-1-61448-899-6 audio
ISBN 978-1-61448-900-9 hardcover
Library of Congress Control Number:
2013957033

Original art by:
Lindsay Moreno

Cover Design by:
Chris Treccani
www.3dogdesign.net

Interior Design by:
Bonnie Bushman
bonnie@caboodlegraphics.com

In an effort to support local communities, raise awareness and funds, Morgan James Publishing donates a percentage of all book sales for the life of each book to Habitat for Humanity Peninsula and Greater Williamsburg.

Get involved today, visit
www.MorganJamesBuilds.com

Habitat
for Humanity®
Peninsula and
Greater Williamsburg
Building Partner

Dedication

I would like to dedicate this book to my mother, Linda. When I was a small child, and the only child at that, she would tell me, "Make your room look like a model home!" And that is where it all began.

She must have known I had a thing for design. I'd spend hours upon hours creating and modifying my homemade Barbie houses. I would cover my entire bedroom floor with Barbie's house. I didn't really care where Barbie and her sisters or her friends were. Every chance I had, I would build and remodel her abode with boxes, small suitcases and just about anything that would stand upright on its own. My favorite was a small, hard-sided suitcase that housed my grandmother's old hairdryer. Stripped of the plastic hood and hose, it was perfect turned on its side to create a walk-in closet, well before we even had one in our home. Yes, that was pretty forward thinking for a 6 year old!

I remember making tiny home fashion and decor magazines complete with covers and scribbled pages. I would carefully place them on the modern tables made from upside-down tissue boxes. Wallpaper was much more challenging, but when I colored clear tape and then cut my designs, I could stick my designs directly on the walls. It was much easier than papering! I think I may have invented wall decals -- I should have taken this trip down memory lane sooner!

When attempting to make my own room a "model home," I remembered all those long days with my parents, traipsing through open houses and model homes and picking "my room" in every home we would tour. I remember wondering, "Why would we look at houses we aren't even going to buy?" and wanting some part of each of the homes that we'd see. After our seemingly long days of idea gathering, my dad would occasionally try to implement something that seemed "easy" to recreate in our home.

In particular, I remember watching my dad, uncle and a neighbor try to stick very trendy, gold-veined square mirrors on the wall in the most professional way a lawyer, a steel worker and a real estate agent could. I watched as the broken squares piled up. And after two days, we had an entire wall of mirrors, which made our family room look huge to me. Of course, there was always the one square that was just a little cracked because the "experts" didn't have the right tool for the job – that was Interior Design Lesson #1. I starred at that one tile every single time I walked by, until we moved, nine years later.

My furniture "designing and manufacturing career" was also totally dependent on the arrival of every new appliance or TV my parents bought. The absolute greatest thing about the first microwave on the market was the box that housed it! It wasn't the space saver microwaves we have now, but rather a huge, noisy and potentially life-threatening device that we all loved. The huge box it arrived in helped me complete my "model home" to perfection. Covered in a blanket and some throw pillows, it made the perfect sofa for my studio apartment home, aka my little pink bedroom with pink shag carpet. I taped a number on the door: Apt. #1. And that is where my design career began.

Thank you, mom.

Table of Contents

Introduction

"Design is not making beauty. Beauty emerges from selection, affinities, integration, love."

– Louis Kahn, American architect

What does your home, and how you look, have anything to do with each other? Can your house really make you look skinny or not so skinny? Believe it or not, the places we live and work – the places where we spend our days and nights – can affect every single element of our lives, including how we look and, more importantly, how we feel about ourselves.

So many of us tie things or objects to our emotions, for instance, when we ask, "Do I look skinny in this (fill in the blank)?" It's such a loaded question that most of our spouses, boyfriends or partners don't even want to answer it, because they know that it's better to stay silent— the smart ones do, anyway. When we feel good about our appearance, it often has very little to do with our physical self. Most of the time, you haven't changed one ounce, your body hasn't changed one bit. In fact, nothing except your attitude has to change to make you feel good about yourself.

Do I look skinny in this house? speaks to the many emotions that we tie to our homes. And that is precisely what Design Psychology is all about. So when I ask, "Do I look skinny in this house?" the question really gets to the heart of how we rely on our home to make us feel, and even sometimes look, a certain way.

The intention behind Design Psychology

Design Psychology is about being intentional in your design, but is also about:

- The effects of color, space and light on how we feel
- The moods we can create with certain looks and genres
- Feeling, flow and function coming together to create fun, family and festivity
- Creating havens in our home – those special spaces and places where we can retreat and get away
- Creating the perfect "aha moment" that we are all searching for when we walk into a room
- Recreating our favorite destinations, vacation spots, family vacations, honeymoons and more.

Design Psychology is really about being intentional about the function and the flow and the form of any room. You will learn a lot more about Design Psychology in your home and your life, with this book. You can also review various terms and definitions in the Glossary at the end.

"Do I look skinny in this house?" will also teach how to create the "aha moment," to understand how your choice of wall color can affect your mood and your life, how important lighting is in your home, the elements of great room flow and so much more.

The heart of Design Psychology

When it comes to design, it seems it's really all about feeling. Even function is ultimately about feeling – when someone creates an office that needs to work on many practical levels, they are still in search of the right emotion, hoping that the room will greet them with, "Hey, come in here and get your work done" as well as the motivation to actually tackle that work.Environments can be motivating and stimulating or they can be soothing and calming – they can create a feeling, mood and atmosphere that makes spending time in them that much more pleasurable, depending on your goals for that particular room.

When I am trying to create an inviting living room, for example, I will work with my clients to find something that truly invites them to sit down after a long day, to relax, to have a glass of wine, to socialize with family and friends, to get closer, to retreat from the day – to do whatever it is that they want that room to encourage. That's an inviting room. And that's Design Psychology.

With some rooms, we are looking for peace, serenity and relaxation. We might be asking our bedrooms or retreat areas to invite us to "come in and relax." We want those walls, floors and spaces to beckon us to take a load off, put our feet up, have a cup of tea or a glass of wine, fall into a deep sleep, relax and watch TV, and enjoy a great book. Design Psychology can do all that and more.

Some rooms, on the other hand, need to inspire action: work, achievement, and activity. These spaces will have an entirely different voice, emotion, function and design. Design Psychology can also do that.

At the heart of it all, then, Design Psychology is about personifying our homes – giving true personality to our rooms and our spaces, so that we feel better about where we live, how our homes function, how we look and how we feel. What we're really doing is tapping into our own personality and all of its amazing facets. Your home has so much to say about you, and it does speak volumes – sometimes it is more subtle and sometimes it speaks loud and clear, but it always has something to say. Think for just a moment about what your home is saying to you right now and what you want it to say. The same thing goes for your office, if applicable. If those two things aren't totally in sync, this book will help you uncover simple strategies and easy-to-implement tips for turning your home into your haven.

Do I need to be an expert in design or psychology?

Absolutely not (although you will probably feel like an expert by the end of this book!)

The concepts and principles of Design Psychology are presented in an easy-to-understand and easy-to-adopt manner in *Do I look skinny in this house?* You do not need any formal background in interior design or in psychology – if you happen to have some, that's great, but it is definitely not required for the successful enjoyment and application of this book.

You will learn how our minds and emotions, heads and hearts are linked, why we make some of the design decisions we do, how to assess your design and life priorities, and how you can spark small or gigantic changes in your home's design and in your life as a whole.

Ultimately, you are the true expert on what you love and how you want to live, and that is what will make you an expert on Design Psychology in your home. And that's all that's required!

Do you look skinny in your house?

The more important question is: Do you feel great in your current house or your office?

Do I look skinny in this house? will help you understand Design Psychology and how it applies to your current home and your dream home (or office). Even more and even better, it will help you look and feel amazing wherever you are. Worksheets that correspond to the many exercises outlined in this book will help you work through the key principles in the book. You'll find the worksheets towards the end of the book.

 Visit Worksheet 1
to write down your answers and set some initial goals.

Chapter 1

Why Design Psychology?

Why do we "ooh" and "ahh" over certain colors, styles, trends and accessories and turn up our noses at others?

Why do some rooms in our current houses completely inspire and invigorate us while others leave us feeling cold?

Why do we spend so much time watching home remodeling shows on TV, flipping through magazines about making our homes more beautiful, and trying to make our houses into homes and havens?

Why?

It's quite simple: Design Psychology.

The who, what, when, where and why of Design Psychology

Design Psychology, the study of design and its effects on emotions and well-being, is all about being intentional with design. It is a combination of life coaching, interior design and environmental design, and it influences our lives much more than we realize.

Design Psychology moves us beyond our basic needs of food, water and shelter – four walls, a floor, ceiling, door and windows – and explains why we want our walls, our rooms and our finishes to influence and perhaps change the way we feel.

What does your home say *about* you? More importantly, what does it say *to* you? What voices do you hear when you walk through your front door and do you like what they have to say?

And *why* is this so important?

I ask myself this question after every meeting with every new client. To this day, I am still amazed that even after all the DIY shows, home improvement stores and magazines, there are still thousands of people searching for the perfect environment and that certain feeling. They are still trying to create the spaces that speak to them. I needed to further understand why there is such a struggle. Why can't we find comfort and satisfaction in our homes and offices – is it so complicated? What is it my clients are really looking for? Is it more than just decor?

Design Psychology goes beyond the *how* – how to update your house, how to paint your walls and how to decorate your living room – into the *why*.

Why do we make the choices we do when it comes to our houses?

Why do our rooms make us feel the way they do?

Why do some spaces make us feel happy while others instantly bring us down?

Why?

Again, it is all about Design Psychology – getting to the heart of our decisions, our emotions, our reactions and our intentions when it comes to design and the places we live, eat and breathe every day.

By applying Design Psychology, you will be able to create a haven and a true "home sweet home," a place that makes you feel happy, fulfilled and alive.

Chapter 2

What Design Psychology is Not

*A*s you continue through this book, you will learn a lot about what Design Psychology is, and how it can literally change your home and your life for the better. To dispel any confusion about this unique and newer branch of interior design, I wanted to briefly share what Design Psychology is NOT:

- Design Psychology is NOT a one-size-fits-all solution. Different parts, philosophies and ideas will work for different people, different spaces and different tastes. Take what you like, implement it in your home and office, and feel free to discard the rest. It IS a solution that can work for you when you customize Design Psychology to your needs.

- Design Psychology does NOT require an advanced degree. While you can pursue higher-level academic studies in the field, that's not really want this book is about. It is more about finding simple solutions to make lasting changes in your favorite spaces and places.
- Design Psychology is NOT black and white – gray is allowed here! There aren't a ton of rules that you absolutely have to follow or risk being wrong. There are a few good ones that you should definitely keep in mind, but it's rarely an either/or proposition when it comes to creating places that feel great to you.
- Design Psychology is NOT necessarily linear. You don't have to go in a certain order (you can even skip around this book to the chapters that appeal most to you) in order to implement these principles successfully. You can do a little at a time, and then come back later and try something else. It IS, however, about creativity, feeling and that true sense of home.
- While Design Psychology is NOT something you'll find written about in most of your favorite magazines, its principles are used by every design magazine, whether they know it or not.
- Design Psychology is NOT just a fancy name for interior design. Rather, it takes interior design a step further to get to the heart of the matter – and that's what I think makes it so amazing!

And now that you've got all of this under your belt, read on to learn more about what Design Psychology IS and how wonderful and inspiring it can be in your home and your life!

Chapter 3

Why Feeling is So Important to Design

hen I meet with clients, we often talk about how a room looks – its design elements, color scheme, layout, lighting and accessories – but quite honestly, we talk even more about how a room *feels*.

I truly believe that rooms can evoke feelings and emotions, which mean that it is incredibly important to give voice to the feelings you want to surface whenever you walk into a certain room.

For instance, when you step foot into your living room, how does it make you feel? What emotions and sensations come up? Joy, frustration, fun, uncertainty?

How about your bedroom? Your office? Your kitchen?

What if your room turns you off? Puts you in a sad mood? Gives you heartburn and anxiety? Makes you want to turn around or run away? While that might be in the case in your current home or office, we can change all of that.

When you create a room, you truly give it a voice and a feel – it is all about being intentional using the guidance of Design Psychology in your rooms and homes. It's about look *and* it's about feel.

Rooms have voice and feel

In my case, I want my home office to have a very strong voice, something that is authoritative and something that reminds me that I need to get x, y and z done by the end of the week. I take all of this into consideration when planning the layout and flow, colors and furniture – everything that I put into (or sometimes more importantly, take out of) the room.

For my bedroom, on the other hand, I love to hear an elegant voice and feel, something that is very pleasant and relaxing and beautiful. Again, this informs every decision related to this space.

When it comes to my living room, I actually want to hear more of a formal voice, something that is refined and adult. While the living room will always be a family space, I need to keep in mind this preference in its look and design.

And my formal dining room actually looks like a library, so it feels very British in nature to me. When I designed this room, I imagined creating a space where a scholar would want to sit and read a book.

Those are the feelings and voices that I want to hear and the ones come through loud and clear in my home.

Simply put, your rooms need to speak *about you* and they need to speak *to you*.

I recently met with a client who gave voice to this notion when she said, "I'd like to give my rooms a variety of different feelings."

She explained in detail how she wanted each room in her house to *feel* and *sound*.

For example, she wanted her laundry room to have a farm-like feel, and so I pictured a sweet country voice when she said that. And then her kitchen is modeled on a French chateau, so I imagined that that room speaking with a gorgeous French accent. All of this information informed every color, item and decision we added or subtracted in her home.

All of these ideas, feelings and voices can help me – and you – create amazing spaces – it's all about Design Psychology in action.

How do your rooms speak to you? And what do they have to say?

When I am designing and looking for the voice of a room, I keep all of these comments and thoughts in mind when selecting design elements and working to create the overall feel of any room or space. When you take the time to give your rooms a voice, they will start to speak volumes about you.

Every room is so much more than just a wall and a door and a window and a floor and a roof. Rather, it's about creating a voice, a feel and personifying our homes, so they speak and feel the words and emotions that we long for.

Our homes are a true reflection of us – who we really are. Our home is where we live. It is where we breathe. It is where we have our families and socialize, work, sleep and dream. Since we spend so much time in these surroundings, it only makes sense that we want to understand them on the deepest level. Start to pay more attention to feeling than to thinking, and notice how various rooms and places make you feel. Feel free to write these down in a journal or on your computer, so you can return to them as you get into planning, organizing and updating your rooms.

That is really the essence of Design Psychology. As a society, we are clearly searching for something to make us feel better, more connected, more alive, more ourselves. When you get more intentional about the voices and emotions within your rooms, you can focus on creating positive, welcoming spaces in your home.

When you can create bliss by walking into your bedroom, energy by entering your kitchen and warmth by stepping into your living room, your house will truly become a joyful reflection of yourself.

And that's why feeling is so incredibly important to Design Psychology and the design of your home.

Chapter 4

A Brief Historical Tour of Design Psychology

elieve it or not, Design Psychology has been around for centuries – we just didn't always call it that. It has influenced interior design throughout the ages. When you look back, you will probably find threads of Design Psychology throughout your personal history as well.

The ancient Egyptians are usually credited with the development of interior design, as they started to decorate their huts with simple furniture and accessories such as painted vases, sculpture, pictures, animal skins and more. Likewise, the more lavish Egyptian tombs showcased gold, ornamentation and objects that – through design – helped to define and distinguish wealth.

Taking that a step further, both the Roman and Greek civilizations also focused on interior and exterior decoration – creating furniture, tapestries, roofs, vases and more that we continue to recognize for their unique beauty today. Again, decorating and accessorizing became a form of pride as well as an opportunity to combine beauty and comfort.

While the Dark Ages emphasized austerity and simplicity in style and lifestyle, Europe led the way from the 12th century on to the French Renaissance or the rebirth of society's focus on beauty, art, design and spaces that made their occupants feel happy, proud and safe, and then on to the baroque, rococo and neoclassical styles – all elements of Design Psychology throughout the ages.

Both interior and exterior design in the United States and Europe eventually started to focus more on personal expression, ranging from minimalism to art deco. Likewise, home owners and interior designers had to adapt to changing technology – for instance, how to integrate televisions and telephones, washing machines and other newfangled machines into a home or office's design without getting overwhelmed by them.

All in all, interior design started as a form of expression, but was chiefly used by wealthier citizens before becoming an everyday trend in the 1800s. While function was always very important, especially in earlier dwellings that were exposed to the elements, art and ornamentation continued to make their mark on design from the earliest days of civilization.

Historical trends with modern applications

Designers today can pull from trends from the past years, decades and centuries to help their clients create dream homes and dream spaces – that's definitely part of the fun of being an interior designer. Likewise, understanding the psychology of our homes and our preferences also helps anyone designing a space better understand it and its dwellers.

Shaped by history, culture, art, technology and, of course, personality, interior design and Design Psychology through the ages can help us better understand the homes and homeowners that came before us and give us so many amazing looks and ideas for inspiration when it comes to creating our dream homes today and tomorrow.

> **Visit Worksheet 1**
> to note your favorite trends and styles
> through the ages.

Chapter 5

Design Psychology Ages and Stages

You might be surprised to learn that the principles and concepts of Design Psychology can follow us throughout our lives, throughout every age and every life stage. While we are more unconsciously influenced by it at younger ages, we can get that much more intentional about Design Psychology and our spaces over time.

Take a peek at how Design Psychology can apply and work throughout our life spans:

- **Babies:** Naturally, babies aren't in charge of the design of their nurseries (although they do have something to do with its destruction some days), however, parents can certainly use Design Psychology principles to create an intentional space for their little ones. What colors make you happy when you see them each day? You can think way out of the pink and blue box. Maybe a soft gray is especially soothing to you and that will make you a more content and calm parent when you are getting up four times a night to feed and change your newborn. Likewise, how can you be more intentional about organizing and setting up the room, so that it both functions and feels good? Design Psychology does not and should not have to cost you a lot of money; you can use multipurpose pieces, repurposed items, and your own creativity and imagination to create the perfect haven for your newborn.

- **Toddlers**: Now that you have more toddler movement and action to deal with, how can you intentionally create spaces in your home, playroom or nursery that allow for additional exploration and interaction? This might be as simple as rearranging a few pieces of furniture, adding some pops of color or great educational toys, or creating a safer house for everyone. You can have a lot of fun at this stage!

- **Kids:** If you have a 7-going-on-27-year-old, you probably recognize that kids start to develop strong opinions and preferences about their environments at a pretty early age. Maybe your child requires a super cool night light that plays soft music, or maybe he adores being in dark, quiet rooms, or maybe she loves being outdoors as much as possible. In any case, how can you bring this childhood inspiration to life to make life more interesting and enjoyable for your child? Childhood creates a lot of strong and lasting memories, so anything you can do to create harmony, peace, fun and joy for your children now will very likely last a lifetime.

- **Teens:** You may not be able to do much (other than get out of their way) to make your teens especially happy right now, but that doesn't mean Design Psychology can't. Help them create the haven they need for a little privacy. Get involved together on a DIY weekend project that involves simple updating of colors and lighting in your teen's room. You will enjoy some time together as well as some grudging approval from your teen along the way. And make sure to take their opinions and preferences into account: You don't have to paint the entire room black, but you certainly add some cool black accent pieces, for example.

- **Adults:** Once you are out of school and on your own, this is the ideal time to put everything you have learned and will continue to discover about Design Psychology to work for you. As a matter of fact, this book was written just for you! Whether you are living in your first apartment or just moved to a 10,000-square-foot home on the water, you can use the ideas of intention and inspiration (much more to follow!) to create the home or office of your dreams. Ask yourself why certain rooms make you feel a certain why, how your home can become more of a haven and what aspects of your personality could be added to your current home or office.

- **Seniors:** Perhaps you are helping one of your parents settle into senior living or are considering downsizing or transitioning into a different living situation yourself. In any event, you do not have to live a drab lifestyle just because you have moved into a different environment that perhaps focuses more on health and safety and less on lifestyle and beauty. How can you incorporate your favorite colors and objects into your new residence? How can you create a special haven in a new place? What is most important to you at this stage in life?

Design Psychology can impact our choices, our spaces and our lives from day one up through our last breath. When we understand the roles that both design and psychology play in our decision, when we get to the heart of the *why* and learn to live with intention, we can put Design Psychology to work for us – creating special spaces, home sweet homes and the best environments throughout our lives.

> **Visit Worksheet 1**
> to discuss what updates you can make for yourself or others at various stages and ages who live in your home or work in your office space.

Chapter 6

No Need to Break the Budget

I f you are starting to sweat dollar signs, never fear: *Do I look skinny in this house?* is absolutely not about busting your budget or convincing you to buy a $100,000 couch (unless you really, really want that couch and can afford it without facing years of credit card debt). Design Psychology can be implemented on any budget and for any lifestyle: You can spend pennies or hundreds or thousands or millions, it's all up to you and your ideas, interests and needs.

This book will continue to offer a wealth of tips that can be done for free or for a very low cost. I'm a big fan of making simple changes – a vase of fresh flowers, a new framed picture, a great throw pillow or two or some other simple accent pieces, rearranging furniture, repurposing furniture – that can be done both quickly and inexpensively. Sometimes this is the best way to determine if you like a new look or trend without dedicating tons of time or money to it – you can always expand and update more later.

On the other hand, if you would prefer to use the services of a professional designer to help you get and implement specific ideas for your home or office, that can also be arranged. Truly, you can spend as much or as little as you like as you turn your home into a haven.

Here are a few tips for simple savings along the way:

- Do your research. You do not have to buy the first chair or rug that you see. Right down the brand name, style and product number, and then search for it online: Maybe you'll find a better deal somewhere else (and some cute accessories to go along with it, since every website you visit is likely to offer just that).
- Check out second-hand stores, estate and garage sales, Craigslist, online bartering sites and other places where you can find some great items for a steal. This can spark your creativity and help your budget go further.
- Set a budget for each project you undertake. It is easy to go overboard once you get to the home improvement or local furniture store. If you have an overall budget and price tag in mind, you will be more likely to stick to your plan and prevent future credit card panic.
- Ask around. If you are struggling with a new trend or how to set up your living room, ask some friends whose style you really admire. It is always helpful to get ideas and inspiration from others. Likewise, Pinterest, magazines and websites can all be great (and free or really inexpensive) sources of inspiration as well. Maybe you and a friend can each pitch in on a project that the other is working on, saving you some time and money and giving you some great bonding moments along the way.

(Truly, home improvement projects can offer many moments of great comedy.)

- Do it yourself. Just make sure that you are well organized and prepared, so that you don't need to hire an expert to fix your project in the end! And if you do need to hire an expert, you don't have to choose the first one you call – you can shop around for the right pro just like you shop around for a bargain.

- Don't rush into any big decisions. If you have spent a full year saving $5,000 to update your living room, then you want to be mindful about how you spend that money and how it will impact the room and your life. Take your time in making big design decisions.

- And remember, it's never about how much something costs. As a matter of fact, some of our favorite mementos are items from childhood that we inherited for free. Trust your gut when you are picking out new items for your home and stick to the things that really resonate with you.

Even though quality generally costs a little more, if something will last you 10 years versus 10 months, it might be worth the extra investment if you can afford it. A few great high-quality pieces can make any room both look and feel great.

Remember, regardless of the size or scope of your next design project, you can do it on budget, on time and in line with your sense of style. And that is what this book is all about.

Chapter 7

Design Psychology the Celebrity

From Nate Berkus to Kenneth Brown, from *Extreme Home Makeover* to *Income Property*, and from HGTV to TLC, Design Psychology is truly our latest celebrity obsession. Design Psychology now stars in so many different TV shows and channels, so many different home improvement stores and product endorsements, and so many different aspects of our lives that it continues to amaze me.

I starred along with Ty Pennington (whose popular spinoff is *Extreme Home Makeover*) on TLC's *Clean Sweep*. This is when home design shows, and the passion around home décor had just started to skyrocket. On *Clean Sweep*, organizer Peter Walsh and I would go in with our handy carpenter, Eric Stromer, and transform two rooms in two days with just $2,000. It was pure magic. For us, the big reveal was always the best part of every show – to see how two rooms and two days could literally transform people's lives and their futures. While the happy families explored their new rooms, we would all tear up. You could see how their lives would be forever changed simply because we had changed their environments.

From there, I starred as the featured designer on HGTV's *Takeover My Makeover,* where I would swoop in to rescue the homeowners from themed hell. Each homeowner had attempted to implement a theme, something that they saw in a magazine that excited or inspired them, but then the entire design somehow went horribly wrong. We would first do an on-camera interview to discuss what they were attempting to do or create. More than the theme itself, every homeowner featured that show was trying to "capture a feeling" in their home. Whether it was a new feeling or whether they were attempting to recreate how they felt on vacation or whether they were harkening back to happy childhood memories, they were searching for emotions in their homes.

Reality TV can truly provide a great window into the inner workings of Design Psychology.

Design Psychology stars on the small screen

As you sit down to watch TV (especially any sort of reality TV), you will likely notice that almost every single show somehow acknowledges the importance of home design and decoration, of making changes to a house in order to make changes on a larger personal scale. It's always more than just the paint on the wall or the new skylight.

It's incredibly interesting to see the way design has influenced other television shows as well. The next time you are watching your favorite show, whether it's *Sex and the City* reruns, *The Bachelor* or *Modern Family*, pay attention to how everything is put together. I always like to notice the wall treatments, which are often used to personify different characters, as well as the colors and the furniture and the way rooms are set up – you name it. None of this happens by accident – shows hire people to design life-like spaces that then take on a life of their own and represent the different individuals who spend time and live in them.

Set design simply uses Design Psychology to create remarkable characters and to determine how they live, who they are, how they interact with others, and how the objects and spaces in their lives reflect various elements of their personality. As you might imagine, it is a (rapidly!) growing industry.

After paying some attention to how a news anchor's desk reflects his or her organization and attention to detail on the nightly news or how Peggy's home reflects her inner turmoil in *Mad Men*, you can then turn your attention to your own surroundings.

How to star in your own reality TV show

Pretend that you are a character on a hit TV show – it can even be your current favorite show. Walk through your own home and have a look at it from another perspective. Imagine some of your favorite characters sitting on your sofas and visiting your living room and your family room. What do your spaces say about you and your character? Would your home make you the main love interest, the quirky sidekick or the difficult mother-in-law? Are you really creating that haven that you're looking for through TV eyes or do you need to make some changes? How could your show be even more of a hit?

> **Visit Worksheet 2**
> to focus on your life as a reality TV star.

You don't ever have to audition for reality TV to see how your living spaces can influence and impact your lifestyle.

Reality TV has real-world applications

When the first design shows launched, I know many of my friends thought, "That is amazing! But I could never do that on my own." Still, they were fascinated and riveted by these reality TV transformations. They were riveted by not only the colors and the designs and the creativity, but also by the psychology behind it: how houses truly make people tick, how rooms can make people feel and how even small changes created such profound differences in the homeowners' lives. When you witnessed a family returning to their home after a disaster, a remodel or an update, you could literally see new confidence and new belief in their eyes and in their actions.

I was just watching a transformation show where they were featuring a business. In order to enhance employee morale within the business, updating the décor was recognized as a key component to change, and that's actually what got everybody rolling in the right direction. Simply updating the workplace environment created a certain sense of accomplishment, a certain sense of change and a certain sense of progression within the office. Whether the business owners knew about Design Psychology or not, they put it into action. They were searching for a feeling and better morale, and they started to find it by transforming the look of their office, which, in turn, transformed the productivity of their employees and office as a whole.

Likewise, I recently took on a client who had moved her office into her home. She had recently been promoted and was able to communicate regularly with her staff via Skype and video conferencing. She told me that she was confused and worried about her new position in her workplace.

When I visited her home to do the routine walk-through, I was able to get a feel for her design style and admired her worldly souvenirs. She had accumulated some beautiful artifacts and hand-made sculptures from her travels. Her home was truly a museum. As we walked to her home office, again, the walls were covered with photos and memorabilia of her adventures. One striking feature to the room, however, was an entire feature wall of tribal masks. To be honest, it was fascinating but daunting and a little off-putting. I took my notes and asked to "meet" with her via Skype, because I had a hunch. Two days later, we video conferenced, so that I could see what her employees and clients were seeing while doing business with her, and just as I thought: I felt as if I were being attacked! When sitting at the computer during the conference, I couldn't pay close attention to my client and her message, because I couldn't take my eyes off the scary voodoo-looking faces glaring intently back at me.

I recorded our call and sent the footage to my client. She was shocked at the image and impression she had inadvertently been sending to her staff. After some simple rearranging, productivity, communication, employee relations and positive responses from her clients all increased within a matter of just two weeks.

Reality TV and your reality

With all of these popular shows in mind, then, it's not a mystery to us that if we are looking for success and fulfillment and movement in the right direction toward a certain feeling and a certain lifestyle, we have to transform our homes to transform our hearts. It is definitely part of the equation and part of the overall transformation process and magic.

It's what everyone walking through Home Depot or Lowes on a weekend is searching for, regardless if his or her list says "pale yellow paint" or "fun shower curtain" or "large kitchen tile." We are trying to match the inside with the outside, so that we feel good and live well.

Design Psychology truly is a celebrity today – and a pretty cool one at that.

Chapter 8

There's No Place Like Home

We all remember Dorothy in *The Wizard of Oz* lamenting, "There's no place like home…there's no place like home." And she was right.

But home can be so many different things. It might conjure up your childhood home – those smells, colors, rooms and feelings you grew up with as you learned the meaning of "home."

It might be your current home. Home can also be your ultimate dream home or just a feeling you get when you hear the word.

Just what is "home?"

Here is how the dictionary defines the word home:

home   [hohm] noun, adjective, adverb, verb, homed, hom·ing, noun

1. a house, apartment, or other shelter that is the usual residence of a person, family, or household.
2. the place in which one's domestic affections are centered.
3. an institution for the homeless, sick, etc.: a nursing home.
4. the dwelling place or retreat of an animal.
5. the place or region where something is native or most common.
6. any place of residence or refuge: a heavenly home.
7. a person's native place or own country.
8. (in games) the destination or goal.
9. a principal base of operations or activities: The new stadium will be the home of the local football team.
10. Baseball . home plate.

According to Wikipedia, a home is a place of residence or refuge. When it refers to a building, it is usually a place in which an individual or a family can live and store personal property. "Home" is also used to refer to the geographical area (whether it be a suburb, town, city or country) in which a person grew up or feels that he or she belongs. Sometimes, as an alternative to the definition of "home" as a physical locale, there is "Home is where you hang your hat." Home may be perceived to have no physical location, instead, home may relate instead to a mental or emotional state of refuge or comfort. Popular sayings along these lines also include "Home is where the heart is" and "You can never go home again." A home is generally a place that is close to the heart of the owner, and it can become a prized possession or ideal.

It has been argued that psychologically, "The strongest sense of home commonly coincides geographically with a dwelling. Usually the sense of home attenuates as one moves away from that point, but it does not do so in a fixed or regular way," according to Theano S. Terkenli, a professor of Human and Cultural Geography and the Cultural Landscape, who has written several books on cultural landscapes.

Trying to capitalize on our strong attachment to home, Sears previously sold homes for purchase and assembly via catalogue.

Creating happy, happy homes

When you analyze the idea of home and what it means, ask yourself what you loved about your first home. Whether it was a beautiful piece of furniture passed down from your favorite grandma, the evocative pictures on the living room walls or a certain mood that your mom knew how to create, there really is a lot of subconscious energy happening every time we walk past a room or every time we look at a lamp that immediately reminds us of something else. If that lamp reminds you of "home," then your body will instantaneously react to that memory.

If the notion of home instantly brings a smile to your face, then items, arrangements and feelings that remind you of that place will likely do the same. Perhaps you love tulips because they remind you of the flowers your dad always got for your mom, or perhaps you are drawn to the color blue because it was the color of your bedroom walls for so many years.

Have you ever gone back to visit a childhood home and felt the same comfort you always did? Do you feel grounded in that space? Do a mental reflection of that space: What design elements do you see? What color are the walls? What kind of flooring do you have in your "home"?

I asked dear friend Dr. Diane Rogers, "How much do you see a childhood home affecting adult choices of home such as sense, look and feel?" She aptly responded, "As meaning-making creatures, we automatically assign significance to experiences. The brain associates these memories with physical places. Our places are a way of seeing the world and reflect our preferred way of being in the world. Childhood memories are important imprints of safety, love and belonging. We bond to places in the same way we form relationships with people. Our sense of identity grows out of patterns of familiarity, congruency and continuity. Our bias for future homes is based on childhood feelings that may reside outside of our conscious adult memory. We know what makes us feel comfortable even though we may not know why. For example, someone raised in a warm climate, who is used to being outdoors year-round, might gravitate toward big, open rooms and prefer spaces with natural light."

One of my clients who recently purchased a home replaced all of the brand-new travertine floors with reclaimed wood flooring, complete with creaks, because that "feels like home" to him!

Recognize these things and, if they do truly make you happy and remind you of that happy home, then by all means, incorporate them into your home today! Small gestures can truly create that home sweet home feel.

Homes without heart

When you really think back to what home means from a historical point of view and how you grew up, you might feel warm fuzzies and you might feel like you've been left out in the cold. Some people, unfortunately, grow up without a sense of home, which is an even deeper psychological topic. If you happen to have items in your current home that remind you of more troubled times, you might want to examine whether you really want those things in your space. Can you get past what that antique lamp from the aunt who always yelled at you represents or does it make you a little uneasy every time you see it? If it's the latter, then turn out the light on such negative feelings and memories.

If you have negative memories or connotations of home, then you need to be very, very conscious that you are not repeating anything or reflecting anything that may remind you of those years or that time in your life. If there was a lot of shouting in your childhood home, for example, then say "no" when your mother tries to pass on her hand-me-down chintz sofa. On a subconscious level, every time you walk past that sofa, you will think of that home and have those same fears and worries that you had as a child.

I have often temporarily removed "negative" items from my clients' homes to illustrate my point. Incidentally, those items never seem to make it back into our final design.

While you don't have to forget who you are and where you came from, moving on and moving through emotional trying memories is healthy. Focusing on the positive and being intentional in your design is the first step.

I have a dear friend who lives in a house that is furnished entirely with items from her sister, who died tragically several years ago. She couldn't figure out why she was feeling so stuck, so unable to move on from her sister's death, even though she had tried so many different methods in her sincere attempts to heal and move past the tragedy. While she thought that surrounding herself with her sister's things honored her sister, the furniture was holding her back. It kept her in a certain state of mourning and a certain state of loss that prevented her from healing and feeling happy. My friend needed to get past the guilt of giving these things away, so that she could heal, move on and find joy again.

It can be nice to honor people we love who have passed by keeping some of their possessions in our homes. I, too, have furniture from grandparents and great-grandparents in my home, but these items are very carefully selected and placed. I focus on the few things that make me smile and instantaneously provide a happy memory. I don't keep things just to keep them; rather I keep the items that evoke a positive feeling of home and happy associations. My dear friend and organizer guru Peter Walsh says we must keep only those things that make us smile and feel content. Honor your family, but know that it is also okay move on.

Design Psychology and your home

Whether you recognize it or not, we all subconsciously know exactly what's in our homes. Likewise, we can all identify rooms that make us feel terrific and rooms that make us feel less-than-delighted. If you have a room, or even part of a room, that makes you feel sad, disgusted, frustrated or any emotion that is at all negative, Design Psychology offers this advice for free: Make a change. And make it now.

Honestly, the willingness to listen to how rooms and things make you feel and to respond in the appropriate way will give you more energy while reducing your stress level. When things look better and feel better on an emotional level, you, too, will feel better. When you are relaxed in a room, you will be more relaxed overall.

If you haven't done so already, take a look around your house and make sure that it is a true reflection of whom you are and how you want to feel. Let Design Psychology help you live better and feel better.

Visit Worksheet 3
to further detail what "home" means to you.

A fun imagination exercise

I have my clients do this fun exercise to understand how our enteric nervous system, otherwise known as the "brain in our belly," works.

Close your eyes, and imagine a morning where you wake up in a beautifully decorated room, with fluffy pillows and the perfect temperature, a hint of lavender in the air and a sense of peace and quiet. Feel that sense of peace and calm in your belly.

Now imagine, waking up in the middle of a damp, dark, smelly, cold garage, filled with boxes, bins, smelly old car parts and broken bicycles. How does your belly feel now?

This is a simple exercise to show how easily we are influenced and affected by the mere *idea* of unpleasantness, let alone truly seeing and experiencing these sensations every day. It is completely normal to have a visceral, subconscious reaction to a design or a room. This is simply part of who you are and what you love – or don't love.

If you haven't already, take a look around your house and make sure that it's a true reflection of how you want to feel and how you want to live. Be sure the items you see every day are giving you the sense of calm and satisfaction that you deserve. Let Design Psychology help you live better and feel better and get more enjoyment out of life.

Chapter 9

Losing a Home in a Disaster

We have all heard the heart-wrenching stories in the media about people who have lost their homes to tornadoes, floods, fires and other natural or manmade disasters. Likewise, we have all seen the photos of devastation and heard of the tales of desperation. While people who survive disasters are grateful for that really important fact, facing the loss of a home can be one of the biggest and most frightening challenges that they will face. That's when the discussion turns more to psychology and a little less to design.

It is important to keep in mind that it takes a long time – physically, mentally and emotionally – to recover from any disaster, whether it's a tree that falls and significantly damages the children's bedrooms on your upper level or the loss of your entire neighborhood in a major storm. Everyone who witnesses or lives through a disaster will be affected, but not all in the same way: Know that it is normal to grieve or feel angry and that recognizing and talking about your feelings of loss or frustration can be a tremendous help. Give yourself time to heal and to rebuild. If others were involved, make sure you take care of each other and offer some time for stress relief every day; children and older adults can be especially affected by a disaster, so getting and providing support is critical for everyone who needs it.

Tips for returning home after a disaster

The following tips can ease your transition if you are returning to your home following a significant disaster:

- First of all, make sure that it is indeed safe to return. You may need to contact the local authorities to ensure that your home is still safe for visitation or habitation.
- Enter your house cautiously, because you might encounter pests or rodents, water or weakened structures, not to mention some strange smells and sights. Use a flashlight rather than a candle for your safety. And avoid returning to your home at night, when hidden dangers can easily go unseen.
- Create a list of priorities. Do you need to clean up or clear out? What is most important to tackle right away? Getting organized will make the entire process go a little more smoothly.
- Keep an eye out for any neighbors who might also need some assistance. Pitching in together can help with both the workload and with the weight of stress and uncertainty.
- If safety remains a concern, make sure you contact a professional inspector before you even open up the front door. You can also wear protective gear, good boots and rubber gloves for personal safety. It is important to check the gas supply, electricity and

electrical appliances, as well as the sewer and water lines right away for safety.

- Throw out food, cosmetics, medicine and anything else that has come in contact with dangerous or uncertain substances.
- Use common sense and seek help if you are feeling overwhelmed, fearful or are struggling to cope.
- And always remember that people are more important than things.

What to do in the case of a total loss

If you are able to return back home eventually, the situation may be stressful, but you will at least enjoy the ability to sleep in your bedroom and to eat breakfast in your kitchen again. However, in the case of a total loss, the mental and emotional affects can be even more challenging to cope with. Likewise, you have to deal with the issue of where to live while you decide to rebuild or move. All of this can take a major toll on individuals and families, so it's important to recognize signs of stress in yourself and the others affected by the home loss.

Following are several things to keep in mind in the tragic event of a total home loss:

- Contact the local and/or national authorities, depending on the event, to discuss the best next steps to take.
- Likewise, contact your insurance company to let them know what has happened and to determine what will be covered, what forms need to be filled out and what other steps need to be taken.
- Get the ongoing help you need from friends, family and loved ones during this stressful time. This might mean therapy, a family trip to your favorite ice cream shop, exercise or a support group.

- Consider whether you want to rebuild in the same place or move to another home.
- Don't rush into any major decisions; rather, give yourself a little time to breathe before you plunge into decision-making. When you do make that big decision, make sure everyone understands the decision and can move forward together.

Finally, if something tragic happens within your home – a death of a loved one, a tragic accident or something similar – you will also need to take into account the effects that the event will have on everyone who lives in the home. This may mean that you need to leave the house for a time, seek counseling or even move on. You might also consider a family ritual that acknowledges what happened, but also gives you permission to let go and find some peace.

Again, everyone can react somewhat differently in the face of a tragedy or home loss, so it is important to be mindful of how you feel and of how those around you are feeling and reacting. Take care of yourself and of each other and remind yourself that home isn't always where you are, but whom you are with.

Chapter 10

Know Yourself

When we don't know or understand what is happening inside, we tend to look for the answers outside. When we seek answers from outside sources, we gravitate toward quick, seemingly great solutions that may eventually become flimsy Band-Aids for bigger problems.

Naturally, this does not always lead to a happy ending

I began working with a client who I will call Shelli. Shelli was well known in her community as a great chef and entertainer. She would host great parties and charity events as often as she could. Approximately two years prior to our working together, Shelli had broken her back, which left her depressed and in constant pain. In her frustration with her physical body, she thought her home would heal her pain.

Shelli had hired and fired four designers over the course of two years, and against all warnings from friends and family, I took her under my wing to try and help her. Deep down, Shelli was a sweet and funny woman who I grew to enjoy. But as her personal problems began to affect the process, she grew difficult, moody and medicated. I knew very early on that no matter what I did, her home would never really be perfect. Shelli had picked out magazine pictures of the reality she wanted to create in her home, but she didn't realize she would never have the home she wanted with so much unrest in her head and her body. It was just easier for her to focus on how her household looked to the outside and what changes she needed to make to that, rather than fixing the reality she lived in.

Maslow's Hierarchy of needs

To take it to another level, let's examine the work of Abraham Maslow, who lived and worked in the early 20th century. Maslow was a professor who founded a major branch of psychology known as humanistic psychology, which examines very personal concepts like basic needs and self-actualization.

Maslow's hierarchy of needs (1943)

Self-actualizing needs — Self-aware personal growth

Esteem needs — Self-worth, accomplishment

Social needs — Belonging, love, family

Security — Safety, steady job, insurance

Physiological — Food, water, shelter, air, warmth

In 1943, he wrote a paper titled "A Theory of Human Motivation" in which he proposed his now famous hierarchy of needs. Over the years, Maslow refined the model into the version that we recognize today:

As you can see, Maslow arranged different types of needs into a pyramid with five tiers: Physiological, Safety, Love/belonging, Esteem and Self-actualization. Different examples of these types of needs can be seen inside each layer, and you can likely identify these needs in your life.

The basic idea here is that the lower the tier, the more basic the need. Another way to say it is that the lower level needs must be met (to a certain degree) before a person will move up the hierarchy. Our personal foundation should be strong enough to support our desires. Our home is in the foundation of our self-actualization; it's the beginning to understanding our true selves.

You need to know yourself well before you can recognize what you want, need and love in a home or office. Take the time to understand and deal with any ongoing issues or unmet needs and to give you time and space to make any changes.

Visit Worksheet 3
to examine your needs on Maslow's hierarchy.

Chapter 11

Design Psychology "F" Words

es, there are actual "F" words in Design Psychology, but they are all okay to say out loud. They are the F words that we say often and loud and proud: function, feel and flow. Likewise, you can say these words as much as you like when it comes to your house, because they all play an incredibly important role in creating the space of your dreams.

F word #1: Function

The first one that we will talk about is function, which relates to the number one question that I ask all of my clients: How will this room function? Since we ask so much of the various rooms in our homes these days, really honing in and focusing on function is incredibly important.

We need to know how the room currently functions and how the room needs to function going forward.

And that's just the start of it. Under function, I also ask my clients:

- Who lives in this home?
- What kind of people (moms, dads, kids, cooks, athletes, office managers, etc.)?
- Are there any special needs for the room or house?
- Do rooms need to be multi-functioning and multi-purpose?
- Are there any other functions you'd like your home to have?

After we address who lives in the house and what happens there, we then make a list – a really honest and thorough list.

For example, your list for your family room might list its function – where the family gathers and hangs out, recognizing that this room needs to encompass a lot of different needs. Then you would list the who – Bob, the dad, loves to watch TV, read, enjoy a cocktail, talk to his kids and to relax in the family room. That means you need to keep a TV, a table for drinks/books/remote controls and comfortable chairs or couches in mind.

Next is Betty, Bob's wife. She is a huge coffee drinker and does not like sinking down into a big couch (so I make a note to self: think comfortable upright chair for Betty). She likes to listen to music, knit, hang out with the kids (including offering some homework help) and host her monthly book club in the family room. So in addition to Betty's upright chair, other important items might include a stereo or iPod hook-up, tables for homework and flexible space for hosting up to 10 people at one time.

Bella, the couple's teenage daughter, primarily wants to use the computer in the family room, where she can do her homework, but, most importantly to her, to watch her favorite reality TV shows. She also hosts an occasional sleepover here where she and her friends watch movies, Skype (and giggle), and she also likes to paint her fingernails – lately her favorite color is lime green. Bella, then, needs space for the computer, flexible space for sleepovers, good lighting and durable surfaces.

Finally, Billy, the youngest, is a video game aficionado. He also uses the computer, when Bella lets him, and he likes to have his afternoon snack (chips and salsa or a granola bar) here. Billy also works on model airplanes and watches TV in the family room. Billy also needs a TV, a table where he can sit and enjoy a snack as well as space for computer and hobbies.

This family room is currently not functioning well, because the family's list is quite long and varied as to what needs to happen in this room and sometimes it all happens at the same time, so now what? This is where most people throw their hands in the air and walk away because they just can't figure out how to do it *and* still make it look good, or the other "F," feel good.

Go ahead and make a list for the next room on your list and start to examine the ways in which the room currently functions well and the ways in which it could function better.

Visit Worksheet 4
to examine how your rooms currently function
and how they could function better.

F word #2: Feeling

Feeling is really what Design Psychology is all about – it's the who, what, when, where and why of designing a space. Everyone in this family wants, and deserves, to feel happy and productive in the family room. They want to feel welcome and comfortable and able to accomplish what they need to.

But everybody really wants to feel like the room is conditioned to their needs. And this is more than just function – each member of the family wants something inviting and attractive, so no matter who it is, everyone can invite friends over and feel happy in the room while also being able to enjoy the room on their own or with other family members. That is the feeling that we are trying to impart along with our function.

Different things will naturally feel good to different people. Bob, for instance, loves the color blue, soft fabrics and dim lighting. Betty, on the other hand, absolutely loves fresh flowers, natural, spa-like colors, warm and natural light, and an open and airy feel.

Bella doesn't really care much about color so much. She just wants it to be cool when her friends come over. This room has to have a cool factor for when her girlfriends hang out, because the house and room are a reflection of her cool family.

Billy just wants to have enough space for his buddies to play video games and the room can be any color (except pink) as far as he is concerned, although he does kind of like orange.

At this point, we have a list of form and feelings, so next we need to talk about flow.

Again, you can make a list of feelings for any room in your house, matching how you want the room to feel against how it currently feels to you. This can be incredibly enlightening!

> **Visit Worksheet 4**
> to examine how your rooms currently feel
> and how they could feel better.

F word #3: Flow

If a room does not have flow – if you cannot get from one activity to the next with ease – then function and feeling won't matter all that much. You simply will not feel good in a room that lacks flow.

It's all connected in a circular way. When function, feeling and flow interact, then the room will work. When any of these F words get off, then the room won't work so well.

To imagine not being able to see how to get from point A to point B in a room, first bring to mind one room in your home. Now imagine putting a chair in front of each of the pathways, obstructing the flow. How does that room feel? Awful, right? It's like a maze, unapproachable and uncomfortable. Imagine a table covering half of the doorway to a room. It not only looks silly to us, but it feels ridiculous.

> **Visit Worksheet 4**
> to examine how your rooms currently
> flow and how they could flow better.

We know that people like to have central gathering places. Creating centers to sit together with proper pathways for access is what feels best. We like mini-destinations in our home; I call it "home vacations." However, these home vacations won't feel inviting if we cannot easily access them.

I actually have a client who purchased her furniture to match the look of her beloved dogs – talk about form, feeling and function! We knew that the animals spent half their day on the sofa, just as much as the adults, if not more. So instead of fighting the dog hair and pulling out the lint roller every night, we just went with it. We actually went out together and bought sofas to match the dogs. That is a true acceptance of function in a room.

Bringing the F words together for fun, fun, fun

Function, feeling and flow need to be fluid and connected during the design and implementation process. They all work together, not apart. Many individuals and families are good at getting one or two of these words and concepts right, but if you don't have all three balanced, then the space will simply feel out of whack, just like a three-legged stool that is missing a rung.

While it might seem complex, the F words create a simpler math equation than many people think. It is all about adding up the priorities, dividing up the space, and multiplying the overall happiness and contentment of each person who regularly uses the room. It's the magic of Design Psychology math in action.

Chapter 12

Getting Trendy

ust like the fashion industry adores orange one season and abhors it the next, then asserts the need for shorter or longer hemlines, I am also regularly asked about design trends in color, trends in style, trends in interior décor – and there is always something to talk about. Of course, they are just that – trends. Trends boost designers and stores alike, and just like the fashion industry, the design industry has to recreate itself every three months or so to offer new looks, new lines, new colors and the new must-have items.

Pantone is the industry leader as far as setting colors and color trends for a season. Their team of experts actually goes around the globe searching for the "in" color and looks as well as new style and color combinations. With their expertise and knowledge, they are truly the go-to for the design industry. Pantone is also recognized as a team of "tastemakers," and every facet of design has a select few of these that we look to for ideas. Ironically enough, tastemakers are also trendy and tend to come and go.

Not every trend works for every person or every home

While I always enjoy observing the trends, which can be very exciting and inspiring, it does <u>not</u> mean I rush out and buy new items every season or encourage my clients to do the same. Not every trend works for every person or every home.

Just like the latest trends in hairstyles, naturally, not everything will work for everyone. If you have a round head and a round face, a short, spiky do is probably not the best idea, no matter how wildly popular and trendy that look currently is. If you're a man who's starting to lose some hair, then growing your hair in the back to meet the season's trend of longer hair is, again, probably not your best bet.

In fashion and in our homes, we all have to make sense of trends and determine what ones work for us and what ones simply don't.

There is nothing worse than following a trend if it doesn't suit you. Just like blue eye shadow looks great on some people and not so hot on others, the same holds true for interior design. If you see something trendy in a local art gallery, in the latest Pottery Barn catalog or in your neighbor's living room, you have to pause, take a deep breath and decide if the trend *really* is for you.

If it is? Great. Buy it. If the latest trend really speaks to you and makes you feel energized or relaxed or whatever feeling you are looking for, enjoy it.Surround yourself in it. It's so important to feel good – again that F word "feel" that we seek in design. If something truly makes you feel great, that is exactly what Design Psychology is all about.

But if not? Pass it by. Trends are just trends and they will change – and fast. Focus on the elements that really do speak to you – for the long term – and make your heart and your house sing.

I love the trendy wallpapers and damasks, but in small doses. So I encourage my clients to take the same approach – don't paper your entire house in one look or one color, because it might eventually drive you, your family and even your visitors a little crazy. Take trends in smaller doses. You wouldn't let your 10-year-old son design your house because he happens to like Power Rangers right now, would you? Or have your teenage daughter create a *Hunger Games* motif for the entire lower level? As a general rule, it is best to practice a little patience and impulse control when it comes to trends – adding in the ones that really work for you and passing by the ones that don't.

Trends come and trends go

My client, Bob, was not your typical client by any means. He loved interior design and spent hours on his lunch hour picking up stuff he saw while shopping. The problem was that after Bob brought his quick pick decor items home, he didn't really like anything he brought home! He would stroll the mall, mesmerized by the trendy interior design store windows. He loved the look they would pull together from one week to the next. Like many clients, Bob thought he could just buy a bunch of accessories, hoping to eventually get that design store look and feel at home. Instead Bob's home looked like a mismatched consignment store stuffed full of old trendy stuff that no one wanted.

We had to start from the beginning and really get to the bones of Bob's design style and what would make him feel at home. And it wasn't what Suzy, the salesperson at the mall, was told to put in the window to make people want to buy those items.

Don't get me wrong, the large design accessory stores are great for offering up ideas and opening our eyes to new lines, colors, styles and shapes. But only after we have settled on an authentic design style. THEN we can buy a few pieces that speak to us, and our true design sensibilities. It's fun to have a few items you can change in and out when you need a change. But the whole space should not be throwaway. There will be no sense of attachment to the home whatsoever in that case.

It is also important to remember the mantra: Think quality, not quantity. One great couch can last you a lifetime and work in many different rooms and homes. Focus on purchasing things that mean something to you, that work with your sense of style and home, and that ideally, will last longer than just one season.

Likewise, there are different trends for different seasons, holidays, regions in the country, religions, cultures – you name it. You can adopt trends that you see when on vacation (buying some beautiful turquoise pieces to add to your home while visiting Santa Fe or some fun Cinco de Mayo artwork that you find at a local festival, for example), in various cultural institutions or friends' homes – it's fun to collect a few special objects that represent great getaways or times.

Trends and your budget

Following every trend and every whim can also be a little hard on your budget. If you are trying to redo your look every year or every season, you might get tired of chasing trends and – even more – of paying those bills. But that doesn't mean you can't dabble in them…

Try a new throw pillow or two, fresh flowers in the season's hottest color or rearranging your artwork in a new shape or style. You can even update an entire room if the current trend is just perfect for you and your lifestyle and you're confident that you will enjoy it for years or at least seasons to come.

All of these simple steps can help you decide if a certain trend is really for you and if you want to invest further in it. You don't have to break the bank to have great style.

Be your own trendsetter

Sometimes, it's okay to create and set your own trends. If you have a variety of antiques from your recent 10-year anniversary trip to Europe, but antiques are on their way out, that does not mean your meaningful pieces have to go into storage for the next decade.

While being mindful about what you purchase and how you place it, you can create trends and looks that speak to you – it doesn't really matter if the rest of your neighbors are showcasing similar looks or not. And a great Design Psychology coach can help you make sense of trends, of preferences and of the items that work best in all of your personal spaces.

Chapter 13

Lessons in Appreciation

*A*re you ready to make a change?

Great!

The following exercises will definitely help you take a few steps in the right direction.

Even better? These appreciation exercises are free – they simply take a little time and energy on your part.

These fun lessons in home, room and object appreciation are something that I like to do with clients who feel frustrated, who are on a budget and who really need to get a sense of how a room is laid out as well as the three F words: a sense of function, a sense of flow and, most importantly, a sense feeling.

Lesson in Appreciation #1

This exercise only entails an hour or two, but it will give you some great information. Here's how it works:

- Pick one room in your house. Any room will do.
- Then, assign an emotion to every item in that room (and I mean *every* single item!).
- Be honest about each item. We don't always realize (or understand) what it is we have in our bedrooms, in our kitchens and in our family rooms.
- If you report feeling happy about most of the items in the room, then that space is serving you well. On the other hand, if you feel negatively about quite a few items, that that room is actually negatively impacting your well-being, so you will recognize that it is time to make a change.
- Consider removing the items that don't make you feel so great. Maybe a few need to go in a giveaway or storage pile. This is a simple way to make a positive update to a single room in just a few hours.

If you end up with some contradictory emotions about certain items, try to go with your first, gut instinct, which, more often than not, is right.

You might be completely amazed at your reactions to things you didn't even know you owned anymore. This is a simple but profound way of illustrating Design Psychology in your home – how each of your spaces affects your mind, body and heart.

Whether you were delighted or frustrated about what you found, the next exercise in appreciation will complement this activity and help you make more room for the life you want to live.

Lesson in Appreciation #2

This exercise is one of the greatest things you can do to get started in Design Psychology and making a change, whether it is something really big or something small. To get a clean start, you need to do just that, so here we go:

- Make sure you have at least a full day to play.
- Then clean out the entire room. Yes, the entire room. Empty *everything* in the room that you want to focus on or redesign.
- Take a deep breath. And then take another.
- Reexamine the space – did you really get everything out of it? If not, keep going!

If you have the luxury of space, it is nice to be able to place things in another part of the house, but you can get creative regardless. If you are working on your family room, open up the sliding doors, because the couch might be going out back. If it's a bedroom, move everything into the hall or bathroom – whatever it takes and whatever it is – put it out. We're only talking one day, so you can probably live with a little chaos, knowing that the end result will be pretty cool.

Once the room is empty, then the fun really begins:

- Stand in the middle of the room and look around so that you can remember why you liked the room in the first place.
- Ask yourself: Why did I buy/rent this house? What were/are my favorite things about this room? Try to think positive: Maybe it was out of love for the structure, the walls, a special window, a nook, the lighting, the molding, the year it was built or the style of flooring. There is always a reason.

- Be mindful of your design F words. Think about form, function and feeling as you examine the room and the items that helped create the space.

When we're looking for a place to rent or a place to buy, we are actually searching for a place that speaks to us, a place that means something to us and a place that feels good. When we fill it up with stuff, overload a room or simply get disorganized, we often forget what it is that we really, really loved or liked about that space in the first place. We forget what was charming about it. Sometimes we're trying to cram furniture into a space simply that doesn't have enough room. Sometimes we attempt to bring old memories and old furniture with us that we really should purge. So clearing out your space really allows you to see what it is that's great about that space, what it is that feels good about that space.

If it feels right, write it down. You will likely come up with about two or three things that you love, and I want you to really focus on them. It might be the fireplace, the texture of the walls, a cutout, a color, the coved ceiling or a beautiful French door. See these things clearly, so you give yourself the opportunity to fall in love all over again.

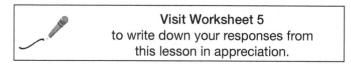

Visit Worksheet 5
to write down your responses from
this lesson in appreciation.

Now:

- Be very, very careful and very, very clear about what you're going to bring back into the space. It might be less than half of what you had before – and that's okay.

- Make sure everything you put back honors the space and what you like about it, rather than detracting from it. For example, if you have a piece of art that you love and you want to bring it back in the room, instead of just hanging it on the wall where it was before, consider hanging it above the fireplace in the most honored place and honored position. It's a win-win. If the French doors are something that you want to highlight, consider putting lovely sheers on them or a light window treatment to draw attention to them, making them more of a focal point than they were before. If you want to highlight your coved ceilings, then paint the walls and the ceiling a beautiful and inspiring color – something that will get noticed. This can be simple and subtle, but can still make a big difference in the room.

- Before you set something down, ask yourself if this is something that you appreciate and highlights the space or something that you're just bringing back out of habit. Be selective and be intentional.

- Notice if any items need repair or rehab – perhaps it's a new covering for your sofa or clean carpets. By bringing back clean, beautiful items, the space will feel more clean and beautiful in turn. A little elbow grease can go a long way.

- Create a giveaway box or an area for the items that you no longer need or no longer love. Take these items to your local nonprofit as soon as possible, before you can start digging back in to the box and cluttering up your room again.

I had a client who recently completed this exercise. Here are her thoughts in her own words: "I went home and I did your exercise. I went through my bedroom and as I was going through it, I realized that my entire family – great-grandparents, grandparents, aunts, uncles, moms, dads, brothers and sisters – everybody was in a frame on my bedroom wall." Then my client added, "What in the hell was I thinking having my entire family staring down at me in my bedroom?"

She realized that if she wanted to boost her romance, she needed to remove the picture so that her entire family wasn't watching over her every night. She truly thought that she was honoring her family, but decided to move her family photos to another room, where they still show her family values, but grandma is no longer staring over her bed.

All in all, we had a great laugh over this, and it's also a great illustration of how this exercise can really change your life!

"The company's coming" game

You know what happens when company is coming over. You start running around the house in a frenzy of organization, cleaning and clearing.

Or when you plan a party, you suddenly decide to redecorate, update and organize every single space that your guests will see.

Why not do that for yourself and your family? Why do we only spend time trying to impress others when we are the people who have to see and live in our homes every day of our lives?

Right now, take a look at one room in your house and ask yourself, "What would I do in this room to update it right now if company were coming today?" How about tomorrow? In a week? In two weeks? In one month? You just gave yourself a Design Psychology to-do list that will make your next party as well as your next day with your family that much better.

Visit Worksheet
to play "the company's coming game."

What do you truly love?

You can give your room or space new life by simply giving it some importance – keeping the things you love and getting rid of the things you don't. You will love the room, you will feel good when you're in it and you will be proud of your space and your efforts.

Highlighting the beauty in your life is a key Design Psychology tip. Really focus on the things that light you up.

These two simple exercises can help you organize, prioritize and really remember what you liked – or didn't like – about a space to begin with. Dedicate a couple hours or a weekend to these lessons in appreciation and you will gain a greater sense of appreciation for the spaces and places in which you live, breathe, move, enjoy, work and relax.

Chapter 14

Quick Fix Tips

Beyond the clean sweep, which can be incredibly energizing and invigorating for both you and your house, you can give your spaces new life with some Design Psychology quick fix tips that won't cost a bundle or require an entire day. Sometimes small changes can add up to big results.

Here are my favorite quick fix tips to spruce up any space:

- Change the lighting. This is one of the least expensive ways to give an area an entirely new look. A simple lamp in a different style – traditional, transitional or modern – can change the entire look and the feel of the space. If you are looking for more of a bargain, just change the lamp shade.

- Get inspired by the natural world. It's very natural and refreshing to take pleasure from natural beauty and design details that emulate nature, such as woven sea grass wallpapers, woods and granites. Focus on adding in a few items that make your house feel a little more homey and natural, even if it's just a fresh-cut bouquet of flowers each week.
- Focus on flow, the third F, and furniture, yet another F. When you identify the natural focal point of a room, you can start to center and arrange your furniture in order to make those focal points pop. This will make your room functional *and* it will feel good. With that in mind, you need to think about how much furniture is in any given room, since it is the number one thing that affects flow. You really don't want your living room to look like a furniture store, so having a space plan is important.
- Build passageways. Think of your room as a maze, so you can figure out how to get around furniture – in front of it or behind it. Creating separation and creating ways to get in and out of vignettes is key for good design and flow. We all know how it feels to be stuck in a restaurant booth when we desperately need to use the restroom but can't get out.
- Remember that entryways are your friends, so you don't want to block them. Keep your furniture about three feet from any entryway, if possible, to create better flow in your home.

I just finished a very small and very fantastic place for a new client. It was a one-bedroom condo with great bones or structure as well as great natural light. However, there was one entryway that caused anyone who walked through it to walk smack dab into the back of a sofa. The place was small. The main living room really needed to be everything – the lounge, the office, the dining room and the entertainment space.After talking with my client about his wish list, I understand that he really wanted a chaise where he could watch TV and entertain others. Since space was at a premium, we settled on a modular piece with an oversized ottoman that could be moved around to provide seating for up to four. Even better, my client and his guests could all walk through the doorways and into the living room without bumping into anything or each other. Just that one change made a huge difference in the function, feel and flow of the room.

Ancient meets modern

An ancient Chinese philosopher, Wabi Sabi, emerged during the Zen dynasty, and his philosophy aligns especially well with today's Design Psychology principles. Wabi Sabi's philosophy was all about simplifying your life and your home by focusing on the pieces that really matter and that really mean something to you.

When you take the time to go through your current living space and choose the best pieces that genuinely mean something to you, the pieces that give you a positive feeling and positive reinforcement, those are the pieces that belong in your home. Those are the pieces that you need to bring in and make important regardless of their monetary value and regardless of current trends. Remember, you can always set your own trends.

Learning to appreciate what you have without a relentless pursuit of perfection is huge, because it all relates to how you feel and what makes you feel good. If you're taking a page out of Wabi Sabi's design principles, then you're actually learning to love what you have – the simple and clean. Your home does not have look like the cover of the latest *Architectural Digest* in order to make you feel good.

Let your love shine through

When you love your home, that feeling will shine through into your day-to-day activities, to your family, friends and other visitors, and to your overall level of comfort, happiness and enjoyment in your space.

I am always impressed when I walk into a home that doesn't look picture perfect or designed by a pro, but where everyone's happy and healthy and the home truly feels alive. It's well-loved and well-used. Every inch has a story and a memory and you instantly feel welcome. People often apologize for their home and that makes me uncomfortable. A happy home, no matter how the interior looks, is a perfectly designed home.

A few quick fixes and simple changes can create a happier home that functions better for everyone.

Chapter 15

House Lust: The Model Home Syndrome

ouse lust – we definitely have it in the United States today!
We are absolutely fascinated with our homes, as well as with other people's homes, magazines on homes, and homes for sale. We have seen the emergence of entire networks that are dedicated to homes and home styles and home sizes and home décor. The number of new house-related shows each year is pretty astounding.

While homes have always been iconic in our society, our sense of house lust truly seems to be at an all-time high.

We tend to express our passion for capitalism through our possessions, so over time, our cars got bigger and bigger and our homes got bigger and bigger. In the 1990s, it was very easy to buy and sell homes with low interest rates and ridiculous mortgages, so then it became easier than ever to acquire more square footage to go along with our giant SUVs, dream vacations, luxurious pools, watches, you name it. With people making so much money on their previous homes, the search for a new home became less about surroundings and feeling comfortable, settled and rooted and more about making money and showing off.

Even though our homes have always been a status symbol, this focus has really mushroomed over the past few decades.

Our obsession with our homes

My friend Daniel McGinn wrote an entire book on this phenomenon called *House Lust: America's Obsession with Our Homes*. He traveled the country to uncover why we are so obsessed with our homes and how people were reacting in challenging economic times. After you finish *Do I look skinny in this house?*, I definitely recommend reading this book!

The name of my book was somewhat inspired by this book and this phenomenon. Today, if you are doing well, according to some people's standards, you have to have a skinny body and a huge house. Is that really what life is all about? Is there more to it?

There is a complicated mix of factors that drive us to really live large. Previously, smart young couples were taught to not buy beyond their means and to avoid being "house poor." If you spend all of your money on a house and can't afford to go out to eat, can't take a vacation, can't even buy a new pair of shoes, and you might start to even resent that dream house.

As we moved into the early '90s, we saw many more house poor couples as dwellings became more and more of a status symbol. The attitude seemed to be: Forget the fact that we can't afford to go out anymore. Forget the fact that we can't afford to vacation. We are going to have everybody come to our house and we are going to have a big party, so everyone can see and marvel at our house. Not our *home* but our *house*.

The word "house" versus the word "home" is a key difference in terminology:

house　　[n., adj. hous] noun, plural hous·es
a.　building in <u>which</u> people live; residence for human beings.

versus

home　　[hohm] noun, adjective, adverb, verb, homed, hom·ing. noun
1.　a house, apartment, or other shelter that is the usual residence of a person, family, or household.
2.　the place in <u>which</u> one's <u>domestic</u> affections are centered.

Bigger is not always better

I am hoping, however, that we are starting to usher in a new era of humility and modesty where we can really focus on the things that are important in our homes rather than just the size of them and of the house itself. As many homeowners now know, bigger is not always better.

Another driving force in the hunt for bigger homes was the supply. New homes and developments were popping up left and right. When I was newly married with two young kids, we moved from a condo to a house on the golf course in less than two years and then moved to a bigger house up the street less than two years after that. We were moving on and moving up, but at what cost?

Also, everyone wanted their home to look exactly like the model homes they would see, forgetting that these homes can cost an additional $200,000 due to all of the fancy extra upgrades. Then they would move in and feel disappointed, suffering from buyer's remorse, because their new home looked nothing like the model they had seen, longed for and toured endlessly. I can't tell you how many phone calls I received from people who had just purchased a home in a newly formed, newly cut area and then suddenly realized that nothing came along with the house. It didn't look anything like what they were led to believe it would look like after visiting all of the model homes. Everything was an extra. Everything was an addition. Their bubble burst.

It's house lust.

For a long time, as Daniel McGinn puts it, we didn't really know what square footage was and suddenly these measurements became critical. "How many square feet is this?" I compare this to diamonds, when women ask, "How many carets is that?" Size really started to matter, and square footage became a real thing. It was one more thing to add to the list: square footage in the house and the number of bedrooms and bathrooms. It became another way of determining a home's value, based on numbers rather than experience and feel. I never remember my parents talking about square footage!

We got so savvy about buying and selling homes that we knew how much homes cost per square foot. We were that good. It is incredibly interesting to understand the psychology behind home buying – there is a lot more to it than closets, bedrooms and garages!

As we entered the mid-2000s, we hit the market crash and many people, through loss, realized the basic meaning of their homes – shelter.

Many of my clients were either losing their homes or ready to stay put, finally. I was being called to remodel the houses they had decided would become their homes. This is when I realized so many people lived in shells they didn't really like, just like hermit crabs that just picked the free shell, rather than really feeling an attachment to their dwellings. I was being called to make much, much more out their structures than ever existed there before.

Design Psychology and the search for the perfect home

Some of us can walk into a home for sale and see infinite possibilities –
how walls could be removed to open up a lower level, how a kitchen
could be completely redesigned and how the paneled walls could be
painted a beautiful soft gray. Some of us, on the other hand, want to
find something that is completely move-in ready, that won't involve
weekends of hard labor or lots of extra dollar signs.

You're probably not surprised by now to hear that Design Psychology
can help you as you are searching for your next home. If you understand
what is truly important to you, such as, the number of bedrooms,
overall color scheme, the look and feel of the neighborhood, a beautiful
backyard for entertaining, a huge family room where you can all hang
out together, you can use your checklist during the house-hunting
process so that you have better results and ultimately love the home
that you end up buying. Make your checklist of the most important
functions and feelings that you want in your next home or office and
bring it with you during the search process.

Slow down, pay attention, and focus on what matters most

Using the principles of Design Psychology, we have to remember to slow
down, pay attention and focus on the things in a home that are most
important. Layout, flow, function and feel - all the while, hopefully,
remembering the people who live there at the top of that list.

If you think you have a case of house lust, take a moment to pause,
appreciate what you have and determine what you can do with the
house (or hopefully the home) that you already have. Design Psychology
can help you bring more intention into your living and working spaces,
turning that case of house lust into a more mild case of house like. It's
totally okay to watch the reality TV house shows, to tour local open
houses and to appreciate what your neighbor has done to his yard
without coveting what they have or wanting to scrap your entire house.

Chapter 16

Organize to Downsize

I still run into many fans of *Clean Sweep*, which was one of my favorite shows to be involved in and to be on. Not only did I meet and work with amazing people like the great organizational guru Peter Walsh and some fantastic producers, but the homeowners were truly amazing as well. They gave us so much to work with, and they also taught us a lot.

On the show, while Peter and I spent a lot of time going through organization and design with each of the homeowners, we also got to understand up close and personal what was really behind most of the disarray in people's lives. It was fascinating to watch what really happens to people when you start to threaten them with organization and, ultimately, the thought of getting rid of things in their lives that lacked meaning.

It was fascinating to see what people find important and what significance they tie to things. Accumulation and purging of itemsis very, very personal. Even more surprising was to watch a homeowner or client who clearly recognized that certain things and items in their home were not only causing disruption or discomfort, but that they were actually halting the function of their rooms entirely. And even with that realization, many people would still cling to those things as comfort, as a life raft, almost like a compulsive eater, slowly destroying their health, still eating and eating.

Make some room for change

Whenever someone says to me, "All of this stuff has to stay," I have to question how much they really want to change, how much they really want to update, and then why? Why does all of this have to stay? Why is it so important to you? There is always meaning behind our belongings and our choices.

In your own home, you can probably determine the difference between disorganized (something of value that simply needs to be put away in its proper place) and complete dysfunction (something that needs to go because it is holding you back or holding you down or slowing you down).

In the first case, you can focus on getting organized by figuring out multiple functions for certain things. For instance, a desk could serve as storage, space to do homework and a crafting station. This is a much simpler issue to deal with in terms of design.

On the other hand, if you find yourself saying, "I can't get rid of this," or "I can't throw this away" over and over again, then you probably need to take a closer look at your house, at your rooms and at the things in them and determine what might be slowing you down and why you're holding on to so much.

Once on *Clean Sweep* we had a homeowner, Jerry, who was up to his ears in boxes of shoes – shoes upon shoes upon shoes –more shoes than anybody could possibly wear in a lifetime, let alone in a year. The shoes were stored in closets, corners, the garage – you name it, they were absolutely everywhere (but very few pairs were ever actually worn on his feet).

But when we talked more with Jerry, we learned that he grew up very poor with no shoes. In his adult years, acquiring so many boxes and pairs of shoes felt like safety, security and status for him. Rather than donate the shoes to someone in need, he was clinging to this inner child who was afraid to get rid of the shoes for fear that he wouldn't have shoes again. In addition, Jerry tied his success to the shoes and his current level income. He had truly wrapped up his entire life and identity in shoes – boxes and boxes of shoes. In this episode of the show, it was so much more about psychology than about the stuff itself.

Outer clutter is usually a pure representation of some inner clutter, whether it's a recent divorce, death, move or other major issue.

> *"If you haven't seen it, worn it, needed it or used it in the last year, get rid of it!"*
>
> **—Kelli Ellis**

My mantra is that if you haven't seen it, worn it, needed it or used it in one year, get rid of it, because chances are very good that you have already replaced or updated that item. I'll repeat it one more time: If you haven't needed it, used it, wanted it, looked at it, enjoyed it for a year, get rid of it.

 Visit Worksheet 6
to examine the current state of your possessions.

On that same episode of *Clean Sweep*, we also talked with Jerry about the importance of places and the items contained within them that serve us and bolster us rather than bringing us down, which his shoes definitely were. The message got through. And after the show, there were some pretty lucky men in local thrift stores.

As Peter used to say in *Clean Sweep*, "If the things you own actually own you, it is time to change!" Likewise, if the function of your room has lost its true function, it is time to purge! When you can't walk from one end of the room to the other without stepping over stuff, it's time to clean, organize and let go. Take a picture of your rooms and then look at them with an honest eye (if you don't trust yourself, ask for a friend's opinion). Do your rooms currently say, "Come on and get productive!" or "Come on in and relax" or whatever you want them to say? If not, then it is time for a healthy change!

> **Visit Worksheet 6
> to assess what messages your rooms
> are sending to you.**

Being able to donate the stuff you no longer need, use or love to someone else in need is a really wonderful thing to do. I also think that the mere feeling of getting rid of things I no longer need or love is absolutely amazing – whether it's through a donation, a swap or in the garbage, it feels good to clear things out and make more space. You can enjoy a nice tax write-off and make some more space in your closets.

Take some time this week to get a bit more organized, whether it is just one drawer in your kitchen or your entire kitchen, for example. Remember what you love, make sure it's put away in a way that you can easily find and access it, and then get rid of what no longer serves you or that room. You can even create "keep," "toss" and "sell" piles to organize your organizing process. Some people make a lot of money by selling the items (clothes, purses, accessories, furniture, you name it these days) that they no longer want. If you are really, really in doubt about a few items, then put them in a box that's out of the way for a month. At the end of the month, if you genuinely missed or needed those items, they can go back. Otherwise, add them to a keep, toss or sell pile and move on.

And remind yourself again what you would do if you were having company – clean, polish, vacuum and shine? If so, why don't you deserve that same wonderful experience every day? It's your home and your haven, so it's important to create organized spaces that you can enjoy on a regular basis, not just for holidays or visits from family and friends. Make that same impression on yourself all the time because you deserve it.

If organization is simply not your cup of tea, hire a pro for a couple hours: You can either find someone to do the entire project for you, or someone to simply map out a strategy and plan for you to follow. If you know that you will have a hard time getting organized on your own, this is a great option that can pay long-term dividends.

Make space for change! Without organization, all of your other beautiful efforts will be meaningless.

Do it Yourself and Design Psychology

For several years, it seemed like most of my clients wanted to buy newer, bigger houses and decorate them, and then move on and buy another house and another. These days, more and more, it seems like people are staying put and updating their current spaces to make them more functional and enjoyable. Rather than moving on, we are staying home, organizing and deciding how we truly want to spend time in the house we have.

Whether it's adding a home office, organizing years of clutter or remodeling the master bathroom, more and more people are enjoying the process of redoing their homes, remodeling their homes and re-experiencing their homes. With that in mind, we are asking more of our homes than ever before.

Under one roof, we are looking to relax, raise our families, sleep, do homework, eat, watch TV, hold weekly meetings with our small business team, host the book club, cook amazing meals – we expect our homes to do it all.

Because we want our homes to be so many things, we have really seen an explosion of DIY or Do It Yourself television shows, home improvement stores and efforts over the past 15-plus years. In addition, some people love a great project; so DIY is perfect for them. Also the "model home syndrome" and "house lust syndrome" left many people house poor, with a very long list of to-dos and little budget to accomplish the list, hence the growing popularity of DIY today.

> **Visit Worksheet 6
> to assess your capacity for DIY.**

My husband has a syndrome that we fondly refer to as "CTG Syndrome" and I'm pretty sure it's fatal and he will die from it. It's "Call the Guy Syndrome." I'm handy, but I'm only so handy: If I can't do a project within a couple hours, forget it. So what do I do? I call the main guy in my life. While doing DIY projects together can be fun, it can also be a little stressful, so be careful not to bite off more than you can chew here. If you feel like your latest house project is going to create an excess of CTG Syndrome, you might want to scale back, move more slowly or call in an expert in whatever your project is.

Do it your way

In terms of home décor, we are realizing that our homes can be such a source of happiness, contentment and productivity, and many of my clients are reallocating their clothing or vacation funds to spend more time and focus at home. And with DIY, we can do it our way, on our schedule and on our budget.

Some people prefer to do one room or one project at a time while others like to try to do everything at once, depending on your budget and your tolerance for mess (and ability to potentially vacate your home for a few days, week or months, if needed). Our home needs to be the place where it all begins as it functions as our workplace, our eating place, our resting place and where we raise our families, so it only makes sense that we want to get it right.

So that's why Design Psychology is so important – understanding what we ask of our homes and then going through and really dissecting what it means to properly design a home with psychology in mind to elicit that "aha moment." It's an important concept to grasp.

It's that love affair that we are searching for in our homes. It is the accolades and the respect from others that come with our home looking and feeling the way it needs to. Our house is a reflection of who we are, our lifestyle, our family, and our hard work. A little organization on a regular basis will make this a beautiful, long-lasting reflection of the best people, experiences and things in your life.

Chapter 17

Get Down to Work

More and more people telecommute or work at least some time at home, which can seem great at first – I'll get to work on my own schedule! I will have more time to spend with the kids! I won't have to dress up every single day! However, when we bring work life into our home and into our havens, it can make it feel like we never leave the office, and we might even miss the social interaction and camaraderie of the office.

While it is certainly getting to be a more challenging distinction with the ease of technology today, most people do prefer to keep their work and home life separate, so it is important to create very specific work spaces within our homes, whether you have a full room to dedicate to it or not. Likewise, if you are going to be inviting coworkers or clients into your home office, then you also need be mindful about setting that space up appropriately.

Making your home office work for you

When you go about updating or setting up a home office, keep the following items and tips in mind:

- How much space do you have? Will you be in a hallway or a full room? Do you have adequate room for a desk, tables, chair, lamps and a full office or will you be sharing space with others? Space will make a big difference when it comes to putting together your plan.

- How can you establish a sense of privacy? Whether it's closing a door or focusing on noise abatement via screens, plants and music, this is a key element to consider when setting up a home office. Likewise, if your work requires quiet time or lots of conference calls, make sure you have the right office set-up for this.

- Will others be in your workspace, too? If so, your office may need to be more formal or separate, depending on your line of business. And ideally, you won't want people walking through the kitchen, the playroom and up the stairs to get to your office if you work a very professional job. Is there an opportunity for a separate entry or door?

- Do you need electronics (printers, routers, projectors, etc.) and a lot of storage space? Where can all of this go? If you get too spread out in the house, then you will have a hard time getting anything done.

- What lighting options do you have? Any workspace requires sufficient light; you simply won't use it if you don't have the right light. Whatever you can see is what you're going to work on. Natural light is always great, but you can use lamps to create a similar effect.

- What inspires you to work? While your office may need to be professional, that doesn't mean you can't use the colors, objects, styles and designs that motivate and inspire you to be more productive and efficient. You can add touches of home as well.

- What other special considerations do you need to keep in mind? Depending on your line of business, you might require special equipment, a unique set-up, high-tech systems or certain décor to create the right function, form and feel for your home office.

Finally, you might want to tour a home office or two or three, or check some well-designed options out in magazines and websites, to get some more food for thought for your next home office project. If you have some friends or business associates with primarily office in their homes, ask them if you can do a quick detective tour to gather some of their clues to success (and ask them what they like and dislike, what works well and what doesn't quite work at all). Likewise, you can tear out pages, pin ideas on Pinterest, and jot down ideas online or in a journal to spark your creativity and make the project that much easier for everyone involved.

As one of my friends learned the hard way, you simply can't set your office up in your child's playroom! However, even a small hallway can accommodate a nice office space. You can get creative when it comes to office space and keep it very simple in order to accomplish your goals, conduct business and even meet with clients. Take some time to examine the best options for your business and then be very mindful about setting up or updating your home office space.

Chapter 18

The Many Shades of Color Therapy

*a*nd no, this has nothing to do with "Shades of Gray"...but it does have a lot to do with shades of mood and feeling...

How do bright yellow walls make you feel? How about dark brown natural wood floors, or baby blue skies?

Do you believe that just one color can really change the way a room looks and feels?

How about your own attitude and energy?

If you answered "yes," then you are absolutely right!

It doesn't take long to realize that color impacts our moods and our feelings, whether we are indoors or out, which means that color choices are a big deal when it comes to Design Psychology principles and applications.

Color therapy is both scientific and healing

Color therapy, which is also known as chromotherapy, is the science-based study of the effects of color, and it plays a big role in Design Psychology and interior design today. Again, it goes back to how colors make you feel, what memories and emotions they evoke, and how different shades help different rooms function within a home or office.

Ask any Home Depot or Lowes employee what the number one question they receive and you will probably hear, "Can you please help me find a wall color?" or "Can you please help me choose a color scheme?" It is one of the top questions that I hear from my clients as well, and color is something we always discuss at length. No one wants to go back to the store six more times in search of just the right shade of eggshell, and no one wants four walls painted in a shade of brown that doesn't inspire them.

Take a few moments to reflect on the colors of the rainbow, and their many shades, and how they make you feel and think. We all have favorites and least favorites for a reason.

Color therapy and motivations

Chromotherapy can actually help you understand your intentions and your motivations. When somebody says, "My favorite color is purple," there is a reason for that. Most of us have a favorite color as well as colors we just do not like. When we learn a little bit more about our color preferences, then we can also learn more about what color means to us, how we relate to color and how we can actually solve some problems using color – it is a pretty amazing (and fun) science.

Color has the power to transform a simple space into something that is more productive, more healing, more relaxing or more energizing.

Color influences us and affects us both directly and indirectly, whether we realize it or not. Even when your eyes are closed, color is still playing a role in your life and your mind's eye.

Every color has energy and a frequency, something that your body can actually tangibly feel. Believe it or not, your heart rate and your breathing rate can both change when you surround yourself with certain colors.

The textbook definition of color is "the visual effect that is caused by the spectral composition of the light emitted, transmitted or reflected by objects." What it really means is that if you see a red apple, that red apple has actually absorbed all of the color rays except red, so red is reflected and that is what you see. When you see a kid eating a handful of pink cotton candy, the confection has absorbed all the color rays that aren't pink, so all we see is pink. Pretty fascinating, isn't it?

To break it down one more time, imagine that the sun is shining on a banana. The sunlight is white, a rainbow of colors, so all of the invisible colors of sunlight shine on the banana. The surface of the banana absorbs all of the light rays except for those that correspond to yellow, so the yellow is reflected to our eyes, which then sends a message to our brain saying, "oh, that's yellow (and yummy)."

That is the beauty of color science in our lives (and in our favorite foods!).

What is your favorite color (and what does it say about you)?

Learning more about our favorite colors is fascinating and can inform how we design and redesign our living spaces:

- Purple: Associated with royalty and nobility, purple was originally made from a hue that could only be afforded by the wealthy. It still lends itself to a regal feeling in a home or an office.

- Blue: The color of sky, water and infinity, blue has been linked to purity, fidelity and spirituality. The blue in the wedding day chant "something old, something new, something borrowed and something blue" comes from the fact that brides used to wear a blue ribbon in their hair and a blue sapphire in their ring to inspire a faithful marriage. The idea of "feeling blue" comes from sailing lore; whenever a captain was lost at sea, that ship would sail home flying blue flags.

- Green: Symbolic of nature, life, renewal, fertility and home, the word green comes from a word meaning "to grow," so this color is all about rebirth and renewal, one of the reasons green is often associated with spring.

- Yellow: One of the oldest pigments, yellow is sometimes associated with maturity as well as sunshine, knowledge and wisdom. The yellow sun is one of the most important symbols in a variety of cultures throughout history, and has been revered for its divine beauty and power.

- Orange: With energy and enthusiasm, orange is all about vibrancy, which is why we have orange traffic cones and orange vests that attract the eye and the attention. A color associated with autumn, orange can also be used to represent transformation.

- Red: The red curtain and the red carpet and the red velvet rope all create a sense of specialness or drama. The color of fire and blood, which can have both positive and negative connotations, red is one of the oldest colors and it is a very powerful one.

- White: Pure as the driven snow, white is another hue seen often in nature (think clouds, snow and flowers, for example). White often represents purity and innocence in Western cultures.

- Brown: Earth, wood and trees, brown can be used to represent warmth, simplicity and dependability (some companies use brown paper to denote a natural product, and UPS chose its brown uniforms to represent reliability).

• Black: Authority and humility, rebellion and conformity, wealth and poverty, black holds a variety of opposites and connotations within its hue. The color can also represent mourning, mystery, evil, power and professionalism.

And that's just the start of it. Color science is deep, broad and, of course, very, very colorful.

Color does matter

According to Color Matters®, for example, green is the most restful color to the human eye and it also has healing powers. Interestingly, early healers, chemists and scientists believed that colors had such a healing property that they put colored water in glass jars, which they then placed in front of a window. These healers then had their clients and patients sit close to the colored waters to absorb their healing power and energy. Those colored glass jars in the window eventually gave rise to Victorian stained glass, which we are still enamored with today.

In addition, green was formerly the color of medicine, initially appearing in a hospital in San Francisco in 1914 when an American surgeon decided white was too bright and diminished his capacity for close examination. He chose green as the color complement to blood red, and developed a room with green floors, green walls, green towels and green sheets. Through the years, doctors thought green light was helpful in treating cancer, that it was the perfect color for medical equipment and more.

Faber Birren, a well-known color consultant in the 1930s, also studied the effects of colors in hospitals and other industrial settings. For a hospital in particular, he wrote, "Green is one of the best of all hues," because it is "fresh in appearance and slightly passive in quality."

Interestingly, Birren also suggested changing billiard tables from green to purple to make them seem more respectable.

Yellow, on the other hand, can be the most irritating color. Babies cry more in yellow rooms, according to certain color research, and couples fight more in yellow rooms. If you enjoy yellow, however, you can simply seek out a softer tint or shade or use it as an accent.

How does color make you feel?

Let's get down to the facts about color and how it makes us feel. When clients say, "I just want to feel good in the room. I just want to feel calm. I want to be able to relax," their next question usually is, "What color should I paint my walls?"

This decorating anecdote led me to realize that most of us tie a feeling, emotion or physiological transformation to actual color, further showcasing the importance of color decisions in a home or office.

What actually happens is that we immediately respond to a certain color and then we also have a long-term effect related to that same color.

Blue, for instance, can be associated with a calming effect, but also with depression, so it is important to assess your reaction to blue or any color – both your first impression and the way you feel around the color for the long term. If you love a color initially, but get worn out by seeing it every day, you are simply not going to want it on your bedroom walls. In addition, different shades of the same color can also elicit different responses, so a light blue might feel more refreshing whereas navy might make you feel gloomier, for example.

Take a look around your house now and notice the color of the walls. Maybe you loved and were inspired by the robin's egg blue you chose five or six years ago, and perhaps you even selected it for its ability to soothe and calm. But now, you might not even notice it or fail to get that same feeling. That's because we get very desensitized to our surroundings. Just like we don't notice the growing pile of old magazines that we've walked by 67 times as we've gone back and forth between the garage and the living room, it sometimes takes another set of eyes or a very intentional dissection of a room to really see what's going on. Even if the color is really bold and something that all of your guests remark on, you will eventually stop noticing it so much or even turn away from it unconsciously over time.

Simply updating the colors on your walls can help you update your energy, your mood and your initiative. You don't have to repaint your walls every season, but if it's been several years since you've made a change and you're feeling a little lackluster, take some time to revisit your color choices. Think of it as a tour through your own personal color art gallery.

Visit Worksheet 7
to examine your feelings about color.

Color is very personal

I recently spoke about Design Psychology at a women's group and one of the attendees was eager to share her affinity for color. She confessed that she really, really loves color and admitted that the color scheme in her home would probably only appeal to her. Every room in her home was painted a very vivid purple and she had a rental property that was also painted purple. I asked her jokingly if it that property was rented, and she responded, "Yes, it is, but by a like-minded person who also loves bright colors and loves to be surrounded by such a vivid color."

She added that she had become somewhat desensitized to the purple, but said that she really loves surrounding herself in that color, and since she lives alone, it's okay. While some of the other women in the room were cringing, imagining all of this garish purple, it didn't matter: The color purple made this woman really happy, which is what counts when you're trying to create a home and a haven.

And remember, color is very personal. If I were to pick one color and poll every client I have, every single one of them would have a somewhat different response because color is that unique and personal to each individual.

With that in mind, when you are dealing with more than one person in a home and trying to achieve the optimal results for an office, living room or a space that needs to be productive, then you may need to select different shades of certain colors to try to find some balance and common ground. Introverts often prefer softer colors and can feel overstimulated in bright or contrasting environments whereas extroverts trend toward bright, loud, cheerful or contrasting colors.

Personality is very important in color choice, and it's important to consider all of the personalities in a home.

Take a color test

In *The Use of Space: Physiological and Philosophical Aspects,* scientist Richard Keeler compared the EKG results of subjects who were placed in a monochromatic room as opposed to a gray room and noted that most subjects' heartbeats were slower in the colorful room than in the gray room.

While most people would think that monochromatic or gray rooms would be soothing and calming, it actually tends to be just the opposite: We love and crave color.

Try this little test yourself: Go through any magazines you have on hand (try not to steal them from your doctor or dentist or salon) and look for pictures or images of rooms that you really, really like. It doesn't matter what magazines you choose, why you like these rooms or what kind of rooms you're viewing.

Done?

Good. Notice the wall color in each picture. You should see a pattern. I have my clients do this as their "homework" before we meet.

While I don't necessarily ask people what their favorite color is when design a room, because it changes and there are different reasons for it, colors do inform our design decisions.

Visit Worksheet 7
to take the magazine test and write down your results.

For example, I have a client who doesn't particularly like orange. She doesn't like things that look orange on her walls. She doesn't like the paint colors to be too gold, yet she loves the orange leaves of liquid amber changing in the fall and is always inspired when fall comes around.

Again, it's all very personal.

Personally, I like warmer tones and when I think of orange, I think of my coy fish that I love. I call them my little water babies. So when I see orange, I don't cringe. It makes me think of happy things, but do I want to paint my walls bright orange? Absolutely not. But I do love orange pillows and vases and have quite a few orange accents in my house.

You can pull out your favorite colors in different ways by using certain colors to evoke certain responses.

In my opinion, the most fascinating bit of color research was done in the 1930s. Faber Birren, the same color consultant and pioneer who decided green was ideal for hospitals, also worked for the U.S. Army and Navy. His work and massive color analysis also improved safety rates in factories as many inexperienced U.S. workers found themselves in factory jobs during the war for which they had little to no preparation. Due to this sudden influx in new employees, the accident rates in factories increased alarmingly.

Due to Birren's work with factories and their subsequent changes in just paint color, the accident rate in some government plants during the war decreased from 46.14 to 5.58 per thousand. Likewise, his work for the U.S. Navy, which involved color specifications for pretty much everything in the organization, reduced the frequency of accidents by almost 30 percent.

All through color! It's pretty amazing when you think about it.

To his credit, Berrin's globally recognized color code is even acknowledged by the Industrial Health and American Medical Association.

Color in our world

The study of color and its symbolism has been used for so long that we rarely even stop to think about it. For instance:

- Colors have been assigned to certain zodiac signs.
- Flags use various colors to represent nations.
- Different rulers in ancient Greek mythology had various colors assigned to them.
- In the Bible, color plays an important role, with white for purity, for example.
- In the military and in professional settings, uniforms, insignias and pins all use color to represent different things.
- Red and green, complementary colors on the color wheel, are recognized worldwide as the colors of Christmas, while orange and black come out for Halloween.

We tie color to our lives in so many large and small ways.

For example, colors are absolutely huge in marketing today. As a matter of fact, color can increase brand recognition by an impressive 80 percent. For instance, the red and white of Coca Cola is widely recognized across the globe and Pepsi's red, white and blue follows closely behind. These cans and their colors are very easy to spot and identify. That is not an accident.

Heinz, the ketchup manufacturer, really used color to make a splash when they changed the color of their ketchup to green. In just seven months after the change, they sold 10 million bottles of ketchup to the tune of $23 million and couldn't keep up with demand – all for a simple change in color.

Apple is also amazing with color. They put colorful iMacs and iPhones on their shelves, which changed the face of color in technology. And a pink iPod is no different than a blue iPod, but that doesn't mean that we don't gravitate to one color (or insist on having more than one because we are fond of multiple colors). Again, it's the same product, but people love and respond to the innovation in color.

And you can do the same thing in your life! You can add a little pop of color to your walls, your shelves, your clothing, your car – and that new color can change the way you feel, react and interact.

Color can add energy, insight and inspiration – in even the smallest of doses.

Things of color in science

Psychologists have documented that living color does more than appeal to our senses – it can also help boost memory. Color actually helps us process information and images more effectively than black and white, increasing our ability to remember them.

In addition, color can convey meaning in two major ways:

1. The natural association that we have with colors; and
2. The psychological symbolism of colors

For example, when we think of blue, we often think of the sky and the ocean, which can provide sense of calm. With green, we often think of fresh-cut grass and nature, which can also engender a sense of peace and calm.

Understanding how and why colors communicate meaning is incredibly important to the study and principles of Design Psychology as evidenced by the following:

- Psychological cultural associations can include the red and green of Christmas, pastels for Easter and so on. So when you are thinking about Design Psychology, you also need to consider your own upbringing and how you personally think about colors and what they mean to you. What does green mean to you? It might symbolize money to you or nature or St. Patrick's Day or your Irish culture. For Muslims, green can indicate heaven. So just one color can have hundreds of different meanings and associations.

- Then we have political associations with flags. We all know that flags can incite a certain feeling, and yet we have so much cross over: Red, white and blue are the colors of the British flag, the American flag and the Australian flag, just for starters. So this incorporates a certain purposeful pattern into the color to create meaning.

- We also associated colors with mood. If you've got the blues or if you are green with envy, what does that mean to you? We blush pink or red when we are embarrassed and we turn a little grayish when we are sick.

- Shades of color are also important: Light blue has a different power and energy than dark blue.

- Fads also rely heavily on color: Avocado green was really popular in the 1960s and '70s in the United States, and is popping up around the world more and more now. Orange also tends to come and go as a hot color.

It is fascinating to see how things change, why they change and all of the ongoing associations we have with color.

Research has shown that the human eye can distinguish at least one million colors and some people believe that number goes as high as seven million (but who would ever sit through that vision test?). Some of these one million-plus colors are energizing. Some are irritating. Some cause headaches. Some soothe us. Some are simply delightful. With all of these colors and all of these emotions, it is really important to understand color and how it affects us.

Color and appetite

Did you know that colors can make you hungry? If you want to decrease your appetite, surround yourself blue or purple. Simply put, we do not like blue food (think mold), so of all the colors, blue and violet are appetite suppressants.

Why?

How often do you see blue food in nature?

Exactly!

Other than blueberries, we don't typically have a good association with blue food. In fact, it's often something that's rotten.

On the other hand, browns and many shades of reds and oranges are appetizing colors – which is exactly why you regularly see those colors in fast food restaurants: They are energizing and appetizing and occur naturally in a lot of foods that we eat. So it's not unusual for us to find something that's red or warm in color and want to enjoy it.

The same is true of greens and yellows and creamy colors. Those are things that we have on our plates regularly (at least, hopefully you do!): green salad, fruits, vegetables, all those healthy, natural foods. These foods and their associated colors can actually induce salivation and can also change our perception of food.

If we see pink, we tend to think sweet, and you will see this reflected in marketing, for instance in Sweet'n Low® little pink packets and in pink Valentine's Day candy hearts. Color really starts to emulate art in the world of food.

We also have long-time associations with foods: Would you want to eat a purple banana or a green potato chip? Colors can actually inform and entice our taste buds.

At any rate, this is all good information to have if you are trying to gain or lose a couple pounds!

Color me happy

So getting back to that "what color should I paint my walls?" question, take all of this amazing color science into account when you make a decision. Get out the color wheel, photos that inspire you, and paint swatches or samples before you dive into five quarts of red paint. Also, make sure you consider the design F words when it comes to color:

1. Function: How does this room that I want to paint function? Will I use it for work, sleep or play and what colors will inspire those activities?
2. Feel: How do you want to feel in this room? What colors will really give you this feeling and energy?
3. Flow: How does your house or office flow from room to room? Is there a unifying color that you can use on the walls, in accent pillows and pieces, and so on?

Visit Worksheet 7
to evaluate the function, feel and flow of
colors in your home or office.

In addition, research cautions again monochromatic rooms where just one color dominates everything. We need visual stimulation. So it really doesn't matter what color it is —red, gray, white or all pink – if everything in one of your rooms is solid and monochromatic, it will become irritating to you due to lack of visual stimulation. It is interesting that we are actually hardwired to have a psychological response to color.

Color and sense

Vision is truly our primary sense. We need our vision in order to survive, and we process more information through our eyes than through sound, smell, touch and taste. Our instinctual responses come largely through our vision.

There is a condition called synesthesia, when one sense triggers a response in a different sense, which is why we have physiological responses to certain colors. This notion can help you understand why some rooms do not work for you and why some do, and why you have a sensory experience or strong feeling to certain rooms and environments.

In other words, sometimes our senses blend together. For example, just seeing or hearing the color lime green can lead to a sour taste in the mouth.

Another really interesting thing is that physical noise to your ear – high-pitched, shrill sounds – can be offset by the color green. A perfect cross over, this is why you see so much sage green and soft green in spas and doctor's offices or other settings where a soothing atmosphere can distract from any outside noises that might be irritating to clients or patients.

Interestingly, the saturation, or strength or brightness, of a color actually has a greater effect on us than its actual hue, according to research from Acking and Kohl in 1973 and Civic in 1970. In other words, we perceive a strong red and a strong green as equally exciting, but we see all muted colors, no matter what they are, as calming.

I have often gone into client's homes and had to change rooms that were supposed to be calming, like a family room designed for enjoyment and relaxation, because it had bright yellow or bright red walls. While the homeowners may have loved those colors, the vivid brights were too distracting and overwhelming, making it harder to relax and focus. Being bold can be fun, but not necessarily when the bold color takes over the entire room, changing its very purpose.

There's an eye-opening experiment entitled *The Effects of Hue Saturation and Brightness,* where the scientists explored the visual effects of saturation and brightness related to attracting attention. They found that green attracted more attention than any other hue no matter what the background color was, and that colors of maximum saturation and brightness attracted attention within a space, especially colors like blue, cayenne, magenta and yellow.

Therefore, you can use color as a tool to emphasize or de-emphasize interior design features in your home, but you have to remember the long-term use of those colors and how irritating or inspiring they can be. Using bright colors sparingly can be very impactful.

A lesson in color appreciation

You just completed the exercise of appreciation that allowed you to clearly determine what you wanted to keep and what you wanted to let go of in one of your rooms.

What did that have to do with color?

More than you might realize!

Color comes into play when you notice what colors are in the items and articles you kept. Does your favorite vase have an interesting color scheme? The furniture you love, or maybe a painting that serves as a focal point? Take some time to examine the items you kept (and to recall those you got rid of) to see if you notice any themes in color.

All of this will help you narrow down your color scheme (along with function, feeling and flow, of course!).

I have a client who I'm working with now, and we decided to just buy small amounts of paint to try on about 10 different walls, so she could take a look and decide how she felt about each of the colors. It is always fun to see how colors work and come alive on a wall, and you should never rush in selecting paint colors.

I asked her:

- Do you like this paint color when you look at it with natural daylight? How about at night?
- Does this wall color "speak to you"?
- Does it work with the other items in this room?
- What about this color resonates with you? Or what about it is off-putting?
- What else could color do for you in this room?

And so on.

You do not have to be afraid of paint – it is very easy to fix by just painting over a color that you don't love. It is the single easiest element to change in a room. It's fun to be your own DIY celebrity designer and play around with paint and color. You new choice will completely change the feel of the room.

I also encourage my clients to go through magazines, scroll through Pinterest and start to identify colors and ideas that they are drawn to. This exercise will help you determine what it is that you want your room to look like and how you want it to feel, including the colors.

Go through stacks of magazines. Gather together 15 or 20 different magazines and bring them home, flip through them and every time you see something that you like, something that appeals to you – you don't need to know why – just tear it out and set it aside. Let your family help, especially if they are going to be using the rooms that you are thinking of remodeling.

After you have collected a variety of pictures that inspire you in some way, then you can start to analyze them. For instance, you might notice, "Oh, out of the 30 pictures I pulled out, I've got 20 with a light yellow wall color. I guess that's what I'm really looking for." Or maybe, "By flipping through these pictures, I can tell that I must really love the use of black as an accent color." This colorful information will really help you take the next step in your home and your life.

And, guess what? You have just found your color scheme.

Playing with color can be one of the most enjoyable aspects of design – have fun and remember, you can always paint over that wall if you don't like it! Your local paint store is ready when you are!

Chapter 19

Scent: The Nose Knows

I t is amazing how many memories can be conjured up simply through scent.

Maybe when you get a whiff of freshly baked apple pie, you immediately think of your grandmother, who made a perfect pie every time you visited.

Smelling a certain perfume may remind you of your mother or your favorite babysitter.

Perhaps the scent of lilacs reminds you of childhood games in the backyard or buttery popcorn conjures up baseball games and matinee movies.

When I smell anything remotely like Rosemilk handcream, I picture my grandmother. I can smell it now just thinking about it and she comes right to mind. I know exactly how her skin felt and smelled based on just the memory of that scent, with its faint rose smell. So if I add an air freshener in my home with a rose smell, that's going to give me nothing but positive feelings.

The nose does know

Our entire demeanor and psyche can change based on the scents in which we surround ourselves. Whether it's food or cologne or outdoor scents, we all have a few key scents we gravitate towards for one reason or another. Some people absolutely love the smell of vanilla when used in baking or toiletries, and there have actually been studies done on this scent indicating that it is also an aphrodisiac for men.

Experts concur that when you are selling a home, the best smell you can have lingering in the air is a combination of vanilla and cinnamon. If you happen to be staging your house and preparing for an upcoming open house, then you should boil some water with a few drops of vanilla and cinnamon sticks on the stove beforehand. The house will be permeated with that smell throughout the open house and it will smell like "home" to anybody who walks in.

The other night, I caught a commercial for Glade, part of the rapidly expanding scent industry (if this doesn't ring a bell, next time you're in Target, find the scent aisle – you will be blown away by the number of scented products and fragrances available). In the commercial, the principal had a spray mechanism on a timer that she plugged into an outlet, which changed scents to apparently "prevent boredom, create harmony and serenity in her home". Clearly, the scents were amazing because she could not have looked happier. It was amazing to me how they are selling the psychology of a scent – both she and her dog (naturally) were thrilled with the changing aromas. The message was: *This stuff is going to transform your life. It's like a drug that's coming out of the walls.*

Scent has both power and meaning

Second to sight, scent is the motivator that drives us to make buying and design decisions. It certainly drives the perfume industry. The perfume industry is a multi-multi-multi-billion dollar industry and now you know why. It's incredibly important to us that we have those certain scents in our lives and that our homes smell a certain way.

I recently finished the showroom and offices of Voluspa Candles, which is a multimillion-dollar business, built on the feelings that various scents can evoke. During the renovation process, and at the point we moved in, the candle-making equipment, I was more and more drawn to the site. Just to be surrounded by the smell of freshly poured candles was heavenly and alluring. It was definitely the best-smelling commercial job I have ever had the pleasure of designing.

In addition, scent is a very simple and affordable thing to update or implement in your home or office: Take note of any scents currently in your home or that you'd like to introduce and let your nose lead the way to a happier home or office space.

Chapter 20

Light the Way

With the right lighting, you can change the look of a space – inside and out. For instance, think about the lighting in dressing rooms, the light in your kitchen versus the lighting scheme in your bedroom, and the way the same building can look totally different in the daytime and at night.

Whether it's the light fixture or the lighting itself, light affects the ambience and the feel of the space.

Let there be light

Simply put, sunny rooms are cheerful, warm and welcoming. Natural light is a wonderful element in any room, so you should always take advantage of any natural light that you have in your home. Morning light streaming in can start your day out on the right foot and give you that needed boost of energy. Likewise, south-facing windows can warm a room in the winter by letting in direct sunlight while you can always use window shades to provide cooling in the summer. People think better, perform better and feel better when their bodies are in sync with the sun (if you've traveled across multiple time zones, you can probably remember how you felt when you got out of sync), so this is a simple way you can add a pop of vitality.

Indirect light, however, can feel somewhat dull, lifeless and cold. Your wall colors, paintings and rooms themselves will actually look different on an overcast day as opposed to a sunny day. Likewise, people's moods can suffer on cloudy, rainy days. Seasonal Affective Disorder, SAD, is a very real disorder taken seriously by the medical and holistic wellness communities alike. We like the warmth and inspiration we get from sunlight, which helps our bodies produce Vitamin D. Some suffer greatly without full spectrum light. SAD was formally described and named in 1984 by Norman E. Rosenthal and his colleagues at the National Institute of Mental Health.

There are many different treatments for classic (winter-based) Seasonal Affective Disorder, including light therapy with sunlight or bright lights, antidepressant medications, cognitive-behavioral therapy and carefully timed supplementation of the hormone melatonin, among others. Light is incredibly potent.

With all of that in mind, your home and office should have well-lit rooms, whether by sun or other means, in order to create the energy and joy you desire in your spaces.

You can create the same mood throughout the day with different lighting schemes and set-ups.

The basics of light

Before we get too much further, here are a couple quick lighting definitions (you won't be quizzed at the end, but these will help you better understand the ins and outs of lighting in your home):

- A space lit with a large amount of diffused background illumination and a small amount of focused task lighting is what we call a **low contrast** and **low stimulation space**. This neutral lighting arrangement is generally ideal for reading or working. You can see everything, but you're not so focused on trying to create ambience. However, too much diffused light can create a dull, flat environment, which can negatively influence your mood and energy level. Department stores and grocery stores actually use lighting to boost business and create a stimulating environment so customers will purchase more.

- On the other hand, a space that is lit with a small amount of diffused light and a large amount of focal lighting is a **high contrast environment**, with strong patterns of light and shade. This pattern can stimulate mood and energy and create a moody environment – think of a cool restaurant lighting scheme or the lighting of artwork. However, note that the attention will go to the lighting, so make sure that's what you ultimately want.

- **Task lighting** provides enough light to read, work or be able to safely walk through a corridor.

- **General lighting** or **ambient lighting** sets a mood or impression and also provides for safe circulation within a space.

- **Visual interest** is lighting that adds an unexpected touch. A table that is lit from underneath or a fountain that is illuminated are two examples of lighting for visual interest.

These terms will help you better understand the nuances of lighting and make it a little easier next time you are out shopping for new lamps, chandeliers or skylights.

Why does lighting matter?

Lighting can help make the function, feel and flow of any room. You will accomplish more, feel better and, of course, avoid crashing into your favorite heirloom vase. If you have a lot of people in one single room, you may need to consider more lights for different tasks, and it can also be fun to determine what you want to highlight in a room with lighting. (You can also disguise that funny stain on the wall or carpet by hiding those in the shadows – a design tactic that is known as anti-highlighting!)

In addition, studies have shown that people like to face walls that are bright and infused with light; while they don't necessarily want to sit directly in the bright light, they like to see that brightness. False focused brightness can also create the idea of the sun and its warmth, although an imitation.

Bad lighting can also give you a headache, reduce your productivity and make it hard to read – which is less than ideal for a home office, a room that definitely requires sufficient lighting. Good office lighting will boost accuracy and minimize fatigue, so this isn't the space to cut back on lights. Ideally, desk lights should come from the side and avoid any weird shadows on your computer or workstation; make sure that your office is illuminated for your success. Also, high-color fluorescent lighting will give you the light you need without making everything look gray and flat.

Lighting can make every space, whether it is an office, a bathroom, a basement or your bedroom, function, feel and flow better. It will increase your enjoyment in any room and your house.

Light the way

Here are a few quick tips when it comes to lighting your way:

- Dimmers are definitely your friends! You can brighten or darken a room depending on the time of day and what you will be doing there. These are relatively easy and inexpensive to install and give you a variety of options when it comes to lighting and mood.
- Think about the mood you want to create in a room when selecting light fixtures.
- Select light fixtures that appeal to you, so that even when the lights are off during the day, the room will charm you.
- Seek balance. Don't let one fixture or one lighting scheme (too many spotlights, for example) overwhelm any given room.
- All of your lamps and lighting fixtures do not have to match! You can be creative and get personal when it comes to lighting.
- Variety is the spice of light! Try to mix it up when it comes to lighting. Likewise, you do not need to have just one type of lighting in a room. Take a risk and try something new. If your lighting scheme is boring, it will ultimately make you feel less inspired. However, make sure your lighting goes with the overall decorative style and feel of the room.

If you are moving into a home or redoing a room, updating the lighting is one of the simplest ways to make a change and make a greater connection to that space.

Light therapy

Used to treat Seasonal Affective Disorder mentioned earlier, light therapy is very real and powerful tool used to treat SAD. When the days get shorter and darker following Daylight Saving Time, some people produce too much of the hormone melatonin, which can make them feel both tired (but unable to sleep) and sad or depressed.

Light or phototherapy uses a full-spectrum light that mimics the sunlight and helps people produce more vitamin D, which updates the body's natural rhythms and boosts both mood and energy. If this sounds like you, you can talk to your doctor about phototherapy or purchase a full spectrum phototherapy device for your home.

When we understand how light makes us feel, we can use it more in our lives to create the rooms and feelings we long for.

Light, in other words

The Principles of Color and Light, published and written in 1878 by Edwin Babbitt and still relevant today, talks all about the power of light and of color.

In the book, Babbitt writes, "Light reveals the glories of the external world and yet is the most glorious of them all. It give beauty, reveals beauty, and in itself most beautiful. It is the analyzer, the truth-teller and the exposer of shams, for it shows things as they are. Its infinite streams measure off the universe and flow into our telescopes from stars, which are quintillions of miles distant. On the other hand, it descends to objects inconceivably small and reveals through the microscope objects fifty millions of times less than can be seen by the naked eye. Like all other fine forces, its movement is wonderfully soft, and yet penetrating and powerful. Without its vivifying influence vegetable, animal, and human life must immediately perish from the earth, and general ruin take place."

Chapter 21

The Other Senses in Design Psychology

While the senses of sight and smell typically make the strongest impression in a home and in Design Psychology principles, that doesn't mean the other senses don't play a role as well. Taste is probably the least applicable – although you do want a kitchen set-up that allows for easy access, cooking and entertaining – however, sound and touch both have parts to play in the unfolding drama of creating your ideal home or office.

Do you hear what I hear?

Do you love lots of hustle and bustle, plenty of noise and excitement? Or do you need adequate quiet time, where the only thing you can hear is the sound of your own breath and maybe some soft music?

Sound is very important as we intentionally design our homes and offices. Some people work really well with lots of noise and activity and some people will shut down in that kind of environment. So what things can you do to enhance or decrease the noise level in your spaces?

For starters, you can add doors and sound-muffling curtains, sound machines that play noises you enjoy, or CD players or iPod docking stations so you can easily listen to music. You can make more open spaces or choose to create small quiet havens. You can add rugs, pillows and plants to absorb sound. You can simply ask for a little quiet time and even create a schedule if needed. There are a variety of simple things you can do to augment or decrease the noise level in any space in your home of office.

Take your preferences – and those of the other who use and enjoy the space on a regular basis – into account as you create the perfect soundscape.

The perfect touch

A baby's skin, a soft blanket, a cozy sweater – we all have favorite tactile experiences that can bring peace and comfort instantly to mind. What feels good on your skin? To sit on? On your floors and walls?

When we sit on a scratchy chair or couch for even a minute, our skin – and our mood – can quickly become irritated. Make sure you test out new fabrics before you purchase them. Stuck with a less-than-comfortable couch? Add more blankets and pillow to increase comfort.

If you have small children, you might need to make accommodations for regular falls – adding more rugs to your hard wood floors to cushion those stumbles, for example.

And if you are drawn to certain fabrics, you can look for more ways to incorporate them into your overall design scheme, creating a place that looks *and* feels great!

Chapter 22

Get Inspired

I f you are looking for another way to put Design Psychology into action, here is my favorite tip: Get inspired!

I have always found that almost every room has an "inspiration piece." If you go back to those interesting and inspiring pictures that you tore out of your magazines, you might start to notice some inspiration pieces in magazines or online spreads as well.

What truly inspires you?

This is a great question to ask yourself: What inspires you in your house, and in your life? I mean really, really inspires you. What gets your heart racing and brings a smile? What motivates you? What thrills and delights you?

You might already have an inspiration piece in mind, or you might need go out and find it (but that doesn't mean you have to spend a lot of money).

Here is how you can get inspired and put that inspiration to work in your home or office:

- If you already have your inspiration piece, it is likely that it's something that was given to you: It could be artwork, a unique multicolored rug or your favorite bedspread. If the item is colorful, make sure you start with this color scheme first, so that everything else falls in line. Even if you have a pink painted vase, you don't have to paint the walls pink, but you might paint them the muted sage green color that is also in the vase and then use the pink as an accent, possibly in a candle or a pillow or something small. Neutral colors are typically great for walls and our inspiration pieces often have something neutral in them.

- On the other hand, you may need to do some shopping. For example, I was recently shopping with a client and we found this amazing rug for his manly, chic bachelor pad. He had some items that he wanted to feature that were mostly brown, black and sage, so I wanted to find another accent color for the walls that would highlight and complement those colors. We decided to paint the walls gray (he was going for a hotel feel), and then we found this amazing rug with grays and browns, beiges and black squares, which were manly, clean and geometric and really pulled all the colors of the room together, giving it that finished designer look.

- What do you need to get inspired today? Whether it's shopping in your home, online or a local store, take a few moments to ponder how inspiration pieces can work in your home or office.

Design Psychology can help us pinpoint the most meaningful, inspirational and useful items and bring them together in a harmonious space.

What if you don't know what you want a particular room to look like? That's okay, because that, too, can be a starting point. You can start narrowing your options down, and by using the process of elimination, design your dream room.

Inspiration and intention

When it comes to being inspired by your rooms, you have to be intentional. I recently spoke with a group of women about Design Psychology and we focused on the idea of cleansing a room of its negativity. I told them to go into one room, look at every item in the room – everything in the room – the floors, the pictures, the walls, the accessories, the lamps, the blankets, every single item in the room and ask themselves, "How do I feel about this?"

I encouraged these women to be very intentional about the things they surround themselves with day in and day out.

One of the women later told me, "I enjoyed so much what you had to say that you changed my life in an hour."

Her reason?

She had been renting a room from a woman in her home and wasn't allowed, per her rental agreement, to paint the walls. She wasn't allowed to make the room hers and it had always bothered her, but she became complacent as time passed.

She added, "I realized when I walked in through the front door that I just never felt at home. I never felt good and I never was happy to be home. Then I realized how darned depressing that really is and how it has to be holding me up that I don't feel good when I get home. Even when I walk into my personal room, in particular, I don't feel grounded. I don't feel safe. I don't feel comfortable. I don't feel relaxed. I don't feel happy. I don't feel confident, which are all things that I really want." After coming to this realization, she finally decided to move because she realized that, "I need to find a place that I can make my own so that I can grow!" I was so excited to hear that.

Another woman from that same seminar also told me that she loved the discussion, and that I had changed her life in that hour (what a great day!). She went on to say that, "I actually have a lot of stuff. I probably have too much stuff, but I love my stuff and it really makes me happy."

She continued, "I looked at everything in my living room and that's a lot of stuff to look at – all of my pictures, all of the knick-knacks and all of the furniture. I really looked at everything that I had in this room that I loved – EXCEPT for one thing; one really big thing." My eyebrows raised and she added that, "I always knew it subconsciously, but I realized that every time I walked into my living room, there is this huge item that makes me think of *him*." She grimaced.

Her *him* was an ex-husband.

She said, "It's the pool table that I bought him and it just makes my gut turn. It gets in all knotted up. I just think of negative things and it doesn't make me happy."

The problem? She really enjoys playing pool.

So she asked me, "Do I get rid of it? What do I do?" and I simply told her, "All you have to do is change the felt on the pool table," and the light bulb went on. She actually lit up. She realized that by making the pool table her own that she could change the negative memory association and keep an item that she really enjoyed.

Now when she looks at the pool table, it is hers. It's an accomplishment. In this case, it was that simple to change a negative memory and association to a new, positive one.

Finally, I had one more attendee approach me. This woman had realized that everything in her bedroom "was a constant reminder of what I haven't finished and it is just bringing me down."

She mentioned that she had at least a dozen books on her nightstands on both sides of the bed – books that she had started and never finished. Every time she'd go to sleep, she would subconsciously think of those books and say, "Gosh, I just don't have any time. I should finish these books. I would love to know what happens in this story, but I'm just too tired. I am too busy. I am totally exhausted."

I told her that she didn't have to get rid of the books, but she did need to move them out of the room. She needed to unclutter her sleeping space so that she could unclutter her thoughts, her dreams and her confidence.

A little inspiration can inspire a lot of change or very small and simple updates; the key is recognizing it when it flashes and being open to something new.

Inspiration comes in so many ways, from so many different places, people, interactions and experiences. Leave yourself open to inspiration the next time it knocks on your door.

Chapter 23

The Natural World

Did you know that plants and flowers can reduce stress, fear and blood pressure and enhance well-being and problem-solving skills?

Even if you weren't aware of that, you are probably not surprised. Nature is amazing and it plays a real role in Design Psychology. Think about the massive beauty of Central Park, time spent at your favorite lake or in your backyard garden – how does that make you feel? And how would you like to bring that into your home?

Nature brings the outside in

Adding nature to your home, as you will see, can be very simple and very effective.

In addition, plants can:

- Absorb noise
- Decrease temperature
- Lower humidity
- Remove toxic chemicals in the home or office
- Increase positive feelings
- Stimulate the healing process
- Look great and inviting
- And more!

Thanks to all of this, flowers and plants offer an impressive $14.51 per hour return on investment in the work place, according to the Census Bureau.

And you don't have to have two green thumbs (or even one) to bring nature into your home. Following are some inspired tips for bringing the outside world in to your favorite spaces:

- While artificial plants do not give off oxygen, they can still add a pop of green and some inspiration to your kitchen or living rooms. And just a vase or two of fresh flowers can add ambience and joy to any room.
- Place a small plant on your desk or change the position of your chair so that you have a better view of the outdoors in an office or living room.
- If you want to absorb more noise in your home or office, consider placing plants in the corners of noisy or open rooms. They can also provide nice balance to a room's design.
- You can also emphasize your windows, letting the greenery from the outdoors shine in. Do you tend to keep your blinds drawn or curtains covering your windows? Let the light and the natural world in and you will notice a real difference in your mood and energy.

- Frame or place items from a favorite vacation in a vase, whether it's autumn leaves, summer seashells or a springtime four-leaf clover.

- Humans love a window view. Pointing to well-known studies by Ulrich in the mid-'80s, views of landscapes out of hospital windows significantly reduced the amount of pain medication that patients needed and sped up their recovery times. Then, studies conducted in the late '90s showed that even images of real or simulated nature could improve recovery times, although photos of real nature scenes work better. Also, patients with access to videos of nature — forests, flowers, oceans and waterfalls — used pain medicine less often. Nature is truly healing and soothing. Find ways to soothe your soul with natural elements.

One interesting study from a mental health journal found that prints from the well-known artist Jackson Pollock "increased stress in everyone," while National Geographic-like nature photos dramatically reduced anxiety. A landscape painting by Van Gogh "had no demonstrable effect." Within the realm of natural scenes, there are particular types of landscape images that are more restorative. If you have nature photos or are considering purchasing some, take the time to examine which scenes inspire you most.

If you take a minute to walk outside among some green trees, to stick your noise in a lilac bush, or even to look at a picture of some plants and flowers, it likely won't take you long to understand how Design Psychology comes to play in the natural world. By inviting the outdoors in, you will enhance the harmony and beauty of your home. Think about the natural elements and colors that inspire you the most and find ways to work them into your everyday life.

The best of indoor/outdoor spaces

If you live in the right climate and have the option of creating a versatile indoor/outdoor space, you can put this lesson into action and have a lot of fun doing so! You might be able to open up your patio doors bigger and wider so that your living room blends seamlessly into your pool area – you could even use some of the same colors and designs to create this unity or redesign your space so that it directs the eye in that direction. Or maybe you have the option of an outdoor kitchen that gets your whole family outside, cooking and hanging out together on beautiful summer nights. A sunroom with a great skylight, a library with a cozy window seat and a big picture window that opens up are other fun examples of combining the best of outdoors and indoors, nature and your house.

What do you love about nature and the great outdoors? What elements of the natural world inspire you the most? How can you bring nature inside to your home or office?

Chapter 24

The Power of Biomimicry

Further drawing on the power of nature, biomimicry is a design method that seeks lasting solutions to human problems by imitating nature's time-tested powers and tactics: We take clues from nature and then apply them to everyday life. Designing and organizing your space to reflect nature can tie us to the wisdom of 3.8 billion years of natures' success. Simply borrowing nature's look, beauty and answers will create more beautiful and balanced spaces in both homes and offices.

Think about it: Nature has such a marvelous way of working together in harmony – flowers and bees, trees and squirrels, sunshine and rain. One living thing balances another in nature, and the same can hold true in our homes and workspaces.

For example, you can:

- Create groupings within items, such as hanging art and setting up accessories to set up connections and correct imbalances. You can create a symbiotic relationship between objects and create more balance in a room. Hang and frame art in different sizes and styles by using a unified color or frame.
- Offset a picture and balance it with a lamp or an object on a table to create more harmony in a room.
- Try as many groupings as you like until you find something you love – feel free to experiment with this idea of biomimicry in your home or office.

More about function and form

Biomimicry also harkens back to one of our favorite F words: function. Think about giraffes who have evolved their long necks so that they could reach treetop leaves to graze, chameleons who change color for safety and elephants with their amazing trunks for feeding, drinking and showering. All of these adaptations are incredibly functional.

With that in mind, function and form are very important when selecting furniture. Storage ottomans and trunk tables are terrific for families: If you have a lot of people using the family living room, these provide extra storage for games, blankets and other items that can clutter up a room, while also offering comfort when you want to put your feet up and relax. Office seating, on the other hand, should be more firm and upright while office tables need to be large enough to spread documents out on while not so large that they block traffic and flow.

Functional form brings biomimicry elements to our everyday lives.

Biomimicry and the bonus of beauty

In addition, nature certainly recognizes the value of beauty: Flowers have colors, scents and designs that are designed by nature to attract bees for pollination. Likewise, within a home, you can frame some beautiful autumn leaves or place seashells and sand in a vase to provide some natural inspiration. If you love to read, you can make a wall of antique prints a focal point; you could also frame favorite literary passages or paint inspiring phrases on the walls of your library, office or study.

Finally, biomimicry teaches us to be resourceful and to find inspiration in the strength of natural things. Sustainable design is all about doing more with less. Consider repurposing when buying furniture or selecting multifunctional items that will limit spending and make your investment last a little longer and go a little further.

For instance, I recently worked with an expecting client who wanted to remodel her nursery. Instead of buying a changing table that would only be used for changing diapers for a (relatively) short period of time, we instead selected a large dresser that could be moved from baby into toddler and early childhood stages, simply placing a nice changing pad on top of the dresser. Likewise, you can put dressers into closets and use closet and room space much more efficiently in any room. Choose wisely and select items that are classic and sustainable. Form and function are the essence of good design for everyday living.

Chapter 25

Creating Privacy in Homes

P rivacy and personal space are a big deal, especially if you live in a 1,000-square-foot New York City apartment with two other people and a needy cat. Everyone has different definitions of personal space and different needs when it comes to privacy and personal time. While that can make incorporating private spaces a little more challenging, it doesn't mean it can't be done!

For instance, you might need an hour or two after breakfast to catch up, clean up and take care of your stuff, including everything from a weekday coffee date, a business meeting, a yoga class, or just some quiet time to reflect and relax. Your husband might prefer his personal time right before dinner, while your son might not need any private time, and your daughter might need nothing but!

People reflect their need for privacy through words and actions: You can sometimes see it in someone's eyes when they are afraid of a hug or of getting closer, for instance. Others might sit down right next to you on the bus, even though there are open seats and rows all around. Lack of private space can actually increase stress levels in the body, so this isn't something to take too lightly when you are trying to create a happy home or a well-run office. Privacy allows us to relax, to just be ourselves, to get away and to unwind. It also gives us a chance to check in and notice how we're feeling and what's really going on in our heads, our hearts and our lives.

Pass the privacy, please

When it comes to your home or office, you may have to get a little creative in terms of personal or private space.

Can you use a pretty screen in the family room so that your daughter can do her homework and text her friends in private?

Or maybe you can give each person in your family 30 minutes of scheduled private TV time each day?

Maybe everyone can have a sign or a signal that lets the others know that they need a little time alone. According to psychologist Dr. Diane Rogers, "Establishing a personal haven where you can genuinely relax or meditate every day is important for physical and mental well-being. The mind-body connection is real. We need places that allow us to unplug, unwind, and come back to our senses. Spending time in a peaceful place has been scientifically proven to reduce stress, anxiety, and depression and improve overall health."

How about designating a nap room in the office (seriously, this is a big and healthy trend in workplaces today!) that gives people a chance for a 15-minute break in the day, or using taller lamps or plants to create more personal space? The simplest thing might be to talk with your family or colleagues and ask for their ideas and suggestions. Again, some people require very little personal space while others need quite a lot of it. When people feel like their private space has been violated, they can get angry, irritable and unhappy so this topic is definitely worth a public conversation or two.

Chapter 26

Design Psychology and Special Populations and Needs

*A*s you have already discovered, Design Psychology can intimately affect the way people feel and live. It can create a great space or a dark one. It can invite people in or turn them away. It can feel like home or just a house. This is particularly relevant when it comes to designing spaces for people with special needs, whether it is kids with developmental challenges, anyone with a serious illness or injury, veterans, seniors, transient populations, kids and adults with social issues, people recovering from loss and trauma, and so on. The adjustment might be temporary – if one of your kids has a broken leg and is on crutches – or might involve longer-term changes – if one of your ailing parents moves in with you, for example.

The right design involves both functional requirements such as ergonomics, space planning and support as well as creating the idea, look and feel of home. Whether you are helping to settle a loved one into a healthcare facility, senior center or your own home, coming back to the principles of Design Psychology can help you create a better place for that person to live.

Consider the following items when designing a space for someone with special needs:

- What equipment (walkers, computers, means of contact and so on) do you need to have nearby? How much room do you have for it and how can you do some rearranging, if needed?
- Do you need medication, water or other supplies on hand?
- How can you reduce or remove any barriers to movement, communication and access?
- What colors, designs, lighting schemes and natural elements do your "special someone" love? How can you integrate more of these into the space that you are updating or designing?
- Will you need to involve others (carpenters, nurses, social workers, family members, etc.) in the planning and execution process? If so, make sure to consult them before charging ahead, so that you take any special rules and regulations into account.
- What personal touches can you add to make the space feel more like home? This can be as simple as a few framed family photos, a candle with a favorite scent or a child's beloved blanket.
- How can you enhance quality of life for this person? Remember, that function is just one of the three Fs. Form and feeling are always important in the scheme of things, and the space should work well and feel good to the person using it.

You probably aren't surprised to hear that Design Psychology can help spark healing in both institutional and home care settings. The principles you've learned can create a sense of nurturing, warmth, wellness and home to spur faster and further mental, physical and emotional healing.

While you may want to consult a professional when you're creating this type of space or room, it is important to use your heart and take into account the needs and preferences of the person you are designing the space for throughout the process. Making some special accommodations doesn't mean that good design has to go out the window: Incorporate the best of Design Psychology into your special project to get the best of function, form and feel for the special people in your life.

Chapter 27

Let Your Heart Lead the Way to Your Haven

*C*reating a haven within your home is very, very important for your heart. We walk around all day with our heads on top of our hearts, but sometimes we need to flip things around and focus on the heart – how it feels and how it reacts to special rooms, areas and items within our homes.

Whether it's a room where you love to read, where you always take a quick power nap on winter Sunday afternoons, or the beautiful tub where you can enjoy a long and luxurious bubble bath, your heart will help you create your haven. It doesn't even have to be an entire room – maybe it's a small space within a room, a place that you can go to get away, relax and unwind. This will help you create a stronger connection to your home or office.

Havens harken back to childhood

Havens really come from childhood. Think back to that place that made you feel safe, that getaway where you went to escape, play, read or relax – a place where you could just be and where you could be in charge. Most of us can quickly come up with a place, a childhood haven that conjures strong, warm and happy memories.

Ready to have some fun with the idea of havens? Great – let's dive in!

> **Visit Worksheet 8**
> to play around with the idea of havens in your home.

1. Draw a picture of your childhood haven or secret hiding spot (this does not need to be perfect in any way, shape or form!). If you are more of a writer, you can describe it in words (in detail) instead.

2. Ask yourself, how can I recreate this in my house today? Whether it's with books or a light, picture or something else, let your childhood inspire you! (Obviously, you probably won't be building a fort in your living room, but you might create a reading nook inspired by your childhood getaway.) Bring in those inspiring elements of nature when you can.

3. Get to work! Even small changes can make a big difference as you create your personal haven.

4. Once you have created your haven, take a look around, pause, enjoy a few deep breaths and notice how it feels. If you need to make tweaks or further updates, now is the time to do so.

5. And then, soak it up and enjoy! That is what havens are all about.

At the end of the day, what inspires you to say, "home at last" or "home sweet home?" When we have the feeling of comfort and foundation, we are much more likely to feel happy and to be productive in our spaces. Ask yourself this question and make sure you can recreate that experience in your house on a regular basis. Ask yourself and list the qualities you need for this haven. "Do I need soothing colors on the walls, cool floors, plants and flowers like your mom used to have, a big overstuffed sofa in the living room, or a certain color scheme?"

This emotional list will help you create your haven.

A haven for you might be a clean corner of the kitchen where you can create new recipes with the veggies from your garden, it might be the day bed in the library where you sneak away to read every evening, or the porch swing on your back porch where you love to relax and unwind. Havens do not need to be expensive to create or large, they just need to be meaningful and accessible.

Also, events and holidays can help to create happy homes – some people absolutely love hosting events and sharing their homes with family and friends. The whole idea behind a house-warming party is exactly that – trying to create more warmth and joy in a home. If you love hosting events and holidays, that's terrific, but remember to focus on creating that same warmth and magic for you and your family on a regular basis. A haven isn't just a one-day experience; it is truly an everyday option for you and your family.

Must-haves for your haven

How many havens does one girl need? More than you might think!

Following are some quick guidelines on establishing special havens within your home:

- You should have at least one haven for every person who lives in your home (or within its immediate vicinity, including an outdoor garden, basketball court, swing or bench, for example). Havens aren't just for you, but also for the other important people in your life.
- Even better, each person can have a haven, or even two, in each room! (This works better for larger rooms, of course, and requires some ingenuity.)
- Let your creativity flow. In a smaller apartment, for instance, you will have to focus on creating smaller havens, but as long as they mean something to you and as long as they create that feeling of getaway and putting the heart over the head, that's all that matters. Let your kids' creativity flow as well as they help to create their own havens at home.
- Havens can shift over time. Your 12-year-old might love her plush pink getaway now, but in a few years, she will likely need something a little different and more grown-up.

If home is where the heart is, then your haven is what will keep your heart happy. A haven is that personal space of retreat, relaxation and rejuvenation. It should make you feel more like yourself.

Follow your heart when it comes to creating your havens and they will be exactly what you need at the end of a long day.

Chapter 28

Starting Your Own Business

Feeling so inspired that you want to start your own business? Or maybe you have already dabbled in interior design, but want to focus more on the Design Psychology angle? I am always happy to encourage others to follow their hearts into an amazing career path; I honestly feel lucky to wake up every day with the opportunity to work with amazing clients, to offer advice on TV, radio and websites, and to do something that I genuinely love. While some jobs can grow dull after a short time, this field just continues to open up, evolve and inspire me on a daily basis. I love talking with people about what I do and sharing ideas!

Tips for getting started

If you are considering getting into the interior design or Design Psychology business, here are a few helpful hints that assisted me along the way:

- Get the education that you need. Personally, I can't help but recommend the Spencer Institute's online Design Psychology Coach certification, which integrates life coaching, interior design and environmental psychology (I had a thing or two to do with the development of this one and loved every minute of it!). This is a great program for anyone in the fields of design, feng shui, professional organizing or life coaching, and is 100 percent online and self-paced. For more information and to register, you can visit www.spencerinstitute.com/design-psychology-coach-certification.

- If in-person education is more your style, find a local program or something you can travel to that suits your needs and your budget. There are a variety of design programs available across the globe; just make sure you select one that covers the components and topics that you are most interested in. You will also learn more about Design Camp in the next chapter, which is a great two-day, action-packed design camp for adults and a great kick-start for anyone interested in pursuing this as a career option!

- Find a great mentor. Again, this could be online or in person, but try to find someone who inspires and motivates you, who is willing to share some time and advice (maybe in return for your assistance on a few projects), and who can ultimately provide a solid recommendation and help you launch or refocus your career.

- Do a few volunteer projects for family and friends. Once you know which direction you want to go, offer your services for free to family and friends for a limited time. They can provide some honest feedback on your work, you will get some valuable practice in, *and* you can take some shots of your finished work for your website and portfolio.

- Consider developing a niche. The wave of the future is the micro-niche – specializing in one area such as green design or creating remarkable indoor/outdoor spaces, for example. When you have a clear niche, you can truly focus on what you are most passionate about and it will help set you apart from others in the field.

- Promote yourself. No one else is going to do it for you (not for free, anyway). You need to focus on building a website, sending out press releases, writing articles, social media, marketing, building word-of-mouth interest – you name it. When you name is synonymous with what you do in your area, you will get more interest, more media coverage and more clients. Of course, you can also hire someone to do this for you, or find an intern who is hoping to gain more experience in marketing and public relations.

- Be patient. Most changes do not happen overnight. It will likely take some time to build your business; that might mean continuing to work another job part time or just doing design work on the weekends initially. Eventually, you will be able to dedicate more and more time to the career you love.

- And give back. This might mean offering some free hours to a local nonprofit, mentoring others in the field as they get going or collaborating with others in complementary fields. It is always a good reminder of where you came from, where you are and who you are.

I can honestly say that I love my work and my clients and feel lucky to have found a field and a calling that suits me and my talents and interests so well. Best wishes to you as pursue your dreams of a career in interior design or Design Psychology!

Chapter 29

Interior Design Camp for Everyone

(Time for some shameless self-promotion!)

Did you go to camp when you were a kid? Do you remember bonfires and lakes and crafts and cabins? If you have fond memories of camp (and you obviously have a great interest in design), then you are in luck!

Camp for adults?

Interior Design Camp is a two-day seminar I host with memy friend Lori Dennis. Camp includes special guest segments led by local and national industry experts in niche fields.

Camp is for designers at every level of expertise. Our campers include everyone from students to 40-year veterans who all leave

Design Camp inspired and recharged! At Design Camp we don't cover basic interior design skill sets, rather we reveal how to thrive and excel in today's economy! Simultaneously, you'll learn about the latest and greatest from the best in the industry, and get inspired to bring your craft to a new level. We developed Interior Design Camp for adults to share top interior design trade secrets, tips and tricks to help more people perfect magazine-ready designs and places that they will absolutely love to live, work, breathe and hang out in. It is truly the ultimate "camp" experience for adults and was designed for people who are passionate about where and how they live and those interested in this growing career field. Camp is a destination for practical, applicable, real-life design insight that you won't get from traditional courses or institutions – and it's a lot of fun!

More details and information is available at www.designcamp.com. In just two action-packed days, Design Camp will give you a full design experience, including the following:

- Successful strategies for negotiating contracts
- Inspiration from top designers
- Creating your own furniture lines
- Creating your own linen line
- Getting a project published
- Marketing and branding for your business
- Social media success tips and strategies
- How to become a design star and television personality
- Shopping!
- Plus cocktail parties, networking opportunities and more.

Can you attend if you are not a designer? Of course you can! Here is a testimonial from one happy Camper who is NOT a designer.

T.L. writes,

Why I went to camp and will return to another one......

1. *To Mix With Happy People*

    Most conferences and industry events are usually boring. Sure, there are some motivational speakers and interesting things you can pick up. But I usually walk away informed, not inspired. The first thing I noticed about Design Camp was the excitement and enthusiasm of the crowd. Happiness is contagious. As the days went on, my smile got bigger.

    The buzz is still with me, and that's a really good thing because it's caffeine free.

2. *To Infuse New Energy into My Business*

    Inspiration moves us forward, but it's a hard energy to maintain when you work for yourself. The daily work routine can quickly drain away enthusiasm. When this happens, it's easy to get distracted, lose focus, and accomplish less. Sustaining momentum requires continual inspiration.

    Attending an event outside my own industry meant that I entered with curiosity rather than expertise. To arrive without expectations allows the space for eagerness and excitement— qualities that fuel inspiration and make you fearless. Design Camp reignited my imagination and helped me remember why I'm in business.

    Since Design Camp, I have been motivated on so many levels. I have been more productive in the last three days than I was in the three previous weeks.

3. *To Get Practical Business Information*

    Technology is moving so quickly that it's hard to keep up—even for people who are in the industry. Today operating a small business is more demanding than ever. Social media has added a new level of complexity and the trends are out pacing many of us.

Design Camp brought together dozens of experts on important business topics like branding, social media, contracts, and marketing. Their enthusiasm for the topics and their knowledge kept me riveted for two days. Initially, I only planned on going for one, but after getting so much out of the first day, I stayed for the second.

I scribbled a thousand notes. I always make notes. But the Design Camp difference is that I've made use of them. I was able to apply what I learned immediately. Bill Indursky and Phil Pallen had me tweeting away like a pro before the conference was over. Who knew?

Inspiration can change your world and reignite your passion. Mine's on fire now.

Does it sound even more fun than the camp you remember? Great! We know you will enjoy Design Camp and if you cannot join us live join us online, at Design Campus! You can always find more information, upcoming dates, our "Campfire Chat" newsletter and more at www. designcamp.com.

Do you prefer more historical or modern elements in your home and office?

- If you're starting to sweat dollar signs, never fear: *Do I look skinny in this house?* is not about busting your budget or convincing you to buy a ridiculously expensive couch. Design Psychology can be implemented on any budget: You can spend pennies, hundreds, thousands or millions, it's all up to you and your ideas, interests and needs. Many home and office update projects can be done for free or for a very low cost, and many simple changes can be done both quickly and inexpensively. Sometimes this is the best way to determine if you like a new look or trend without dedicating tons of time or money to it – you can always expand later.

- You might be surprised to learn that the principles and concepts of Design Psychology can follow us throughout our lives, from every age to every stage. While we are more unconsciously influenced by it at younger ages, we can get that much more intentional about Design Psychology and our spaces over time and as adults with our own homes. How has Design Psychology influenced your design personality over time? And how do you want it to influence your spaces and lifestyle for years to come?

- Believe it or not, reality TV has some great real-world applications when it comes to Design Psychology. Take a look at the environments your favorite shows create, whether they are indoor or outdoor, comedies or dramas. How do set designers use Design Psychology to enhance a character's personality or send a certain message? And taking that a step further, how would you want your reality show to look? What kind of character does your background create?

- Does the phrase "home is where the heart is" apply to your current situation? The idea of "home" can conjure many positive and negative memories and connotations. As you go about creating your home sweet home, it is important to be selective regarding what you choose to keep from the past. When you analyze the idea of home and what it means, ask yourself what you loved about your first home. What didn't you love? How can you honor your past while creating a home beautiful that you will love living in in both the present and the future? Keep the same in mind for any office or vacation spaces as well.

- The loss of a home, whether full or partial, can be physically, emotionally and mentally devastating. If you are ever faced with this situation or supporting a friend or family member going through something similar, be patient and give yourself some time to let off steam and heal. Do you want to return to the same place or move on? How do you best deal with stress and change? Be honest and make sure that you are taking care of yourself and of each other.

- Examining psychologist Abraham Maslow's hierarchy of needs, we can better understand that our personal foundation should be strong enough to support our desires. Our home is in the foundation of our self-actualization, and it is the beginning of understanding our true selves. What needs of yours are unmet? How can you take care of these needs so you can find greater enjoyment, fulfillment and satisfaction on a higher level? What do you ultimately need in a home or office?

- Function, how a space works, feeling, how it feels to everyone who uses it, and flow, how movement can happen within the space, are the three key Design Psychology F words that we use every day. Each word and each concept is critical in getting a space right; they work together not apart. How do your rooms function? How do they feel to you? And how do they flow?

Some simple organization and prioritization can help you get all the Design Psychology F words just right in your spaces.

- Trends come and trends go. Some might work great for you – whether it's the color orange or shorter hemlines – and some might be a disaster – whether it's the color orange or shorter hemlines. You can always add in bits and pieces of the latest trend – if you love it and it works for you – without changing your entire aesthetic or your entire lower level. What trends do you love right now? What past trends really tug at your heartstrings? And what trends of your own would you like to create? All of these questions and answers can inform the design of your home and office space both today and tomorrow.

- A couple simple exercises in appreciation can take you back and help you recall what you like – and don't particularly like – about your rooms and your home. Dedicate some time to culling through a room or part of a room as a means of clearing out the physical, mental and emotional clutter. What do you appreciate about the places and spaces where you live and work? And what could use a little (or major) update?

- Whether it's lighting or inviting in more natural elements, focusing on entryways or building passageways around furniture, some quick fix tips can go a long way, especially if you are pressed for time or money. What simple things could you do today to update your space in a great way? What quick fixes will work best for your space and your budget? Make a plan and get started!

- Ancient meets modern in the world of Wabi Sabi, whose design principles were all about simplifying your life and your home by focusing on the pieces that really matter and that really mean something to you. What pieces mean the most to you? How can you do a better job of highlighting them? What changes do you need to make to create more simplicity, harmony and joy in your home or office?

- House lust is a recent affliction of U.S. homeowners, buyers and renters, where we started to want more and more and bigger and bigger. With the housing bust of the mid-2000s, more people started to realize the importance of their houses as places of shelter and safety and to focus on making houses into homes. Design Psychology can help add more intention to the home buying and decorating process, healing the house lust affliction. Do you have a little or big case of house lust? What is it, exactly, that you are lusting after? And how can you turn your house into more of a home sweet home?

- In the words of Kelli Ellis, "If you haven't needed it, used it, wanted it, looked at it, enjoyed it for a year, get rid of it." And in the words of organizer Peter Walsh, "If the things you own actually own you, it is time to change!" Regular organization should be part of every house project; it can be as simple as one drawer at a time or one room at a time. Likewise, DIY or do-it-yourself is a bigger trend than ever, thanks to the numerous TV shows, magazines and global inspirations. Feel free to move slowly or to scale back if your projects start to overwhelm you or your family, or call in an expert for a few hours of guidance or assistance with your big house beautiful Design Psychology project.

- More and more people telecommute or work at least some time at home, which can seem great at first – I'll get to work on my own schedule! I will have more time to spend with the kids! I won't have to dress up every day! However, when we bring work life into our home and our havens, it can make it feel like we never leave the office and we might even miss the social interaction with our colleagues and friends. While it is certainly getting more challenging with the ease of technology today, most people do prefer to keep their work and home life separate, so it is important to create very specific work spaces within our homes, whether you have a full room to dedicate to it or not. Likewise, if you are going to be inviting coworkers or clients into your home office, it is important to be mindful about setting that space up. What issues do you need to resolve around creating a home office? How often do you work from home? What are the key considerations in setting up an office in your home?

- Color is incredibly powerful – in nature, in foods and in our homes and on our walls. Chromotherapy, or the scientific study of color, shows the power that different colors and hues can have on our moods, feelings and senses. Take the time to select colors for both big projects and small ones: Cut out magazine pictures of rooms that you love and examine their color schemes; buy several tiny cans of paint and put up several colors on the wall that you're looking at repainting; and ask yourself regularly how the colors in your rooms throughout your home or office make you feel, and if that's the feeling you want to maintain. What colors inspire and motivate you? What colors in your home or office need to go?

- Next to sight, scent is the most powerful sense when it comes to evoking memories and setting a mood. Think about your favorite (and least favorite) scents: What do they recall or remind you of? Scent is also very easy and affordable to update or implement in your home or your office. What do you want to smell – and sense – when you walk through the door tomorrow? How can you make a change to the various scents in your spaces?

- Lighting is an easy way to update the feel of any room, and it also gives you a chance to experiment with different schemes and styles that work for you. Light can make us feel energized or depressed, so it is important to examine your response to different lighting schemes. What types of light do you love? Do you have dimmers in most rooms? What simple changes could you make in the near future to bring more light or interest to your rooms?

- While the senses of sight and smell make the strongest impression in a home and in Design Psychology principles, that doesn't mean the other senses don't play a role as well. Taste is probably the least applicable, however, sound and touch both have parts to play in the unfolding drama of creating your ideal home or office. Do you prefer more noise or less? How can you accommodate that? And what fabrics make you "ooh" and "ahh?" Focus on integrating these into your home or office.

- A little inspiration can inspire a lot of change or very small and simple updates; the key is recognizing inspiration when it flashes and being open to something new. Inspiration comes in so many ways, from so many different places, people, interactions and experiences. Try to leave yourself open to inspiration the next time it knocks on your door. What in your current spaces inspires you? What does the exact opposite? How can you open the door to inspiration a little further?

- Did you know that plants and flowers reduce stress, fear and blood pressure and enhance well-being and problem-solving skills? Nature is truly amazing and plays a real role in Design Psychology. Think about the massive beauty of Central Park, time spent at your favorite lake or in your backyard garden – how does that make you feel? What are your favorite natural elements? And how would you like to bring those into your home? Adding nature to your home, as you'll see, can be very simple and very effective

- Drawing on the power of nature, biomimicry is a design method that seeks lasting solutions to human problems by imitating nature's time-tested powers and tactics: We take clues from nature and apply them to everyday life. Designing and organizing your space to reflect nature ties us to the wisdom of 3.8 billion years of natures' success, borrowing nature's look and answers to create more beautiful, balanced spaces. How can you bring the natural world inside? What about nature really inspires you? And could your next design project be more sustainable?

- Privacy and personal space are a big deal, especially if you live in a small space. Everyone has different definitions of personal space and different needs when it comes to privacy and personal time. While that can make incorporating private spaces a little more challenging, it doesn't mean it can't be done! People reflect their need for privacy through words and actions. Lack of private space and personal time can actually increase stress levels in the body, so this isn't something to take too lightly when you're trying to create a happy home or a well-run office. Privacy allows us to relax, to just be ourselves, to get away and to unwind. It also gives us a chance to check in and notice how we're feeling and what's really going on, meriting a public conversation about what your family and colleagues need in terms of personal space. Be flexible and try to offer options that suit everyone who uses or lives in your space.

- Design Psychology can intimately affect the way people feel and live. This is particularly relevant when it comes to designing spaces for people with special needs, whether it is kids with developmental challenges, anyone with a serious illness, veterans, seniors, transient populations, kids and adults with social issues, and so on. The adjustment might be temporary – if one of your kids has a broken leg and is on crutches – or might involve some longer-term changes – if one of your ailing parents moves in with you. The right design involves both functional requirements such as ergonomics, space planning and support as well as creating the idea, look and feel of home. Whether you are helping to settle a loved one into a healthcare facility, senior center or your own home, coming back to the principles of Design Psychology can help you create a better and more intentional place for that person to live.

- Creating a haven within your home is very, very important for your heart. We walk around all day with our heads on top of our hearts, but sometimes we need to flip things around and focus on the heart – how it feels and how it reacts to special rooms, areas and items within our homes. Whether it's a room where you love to read, where you always take a quick power nap on Sunday afternoon or the beautiful tub where you can enjoy a long bubble bath, your heart will help you create your haven. It doesn't even have to be an entire room – maybe it's simply a small space within a room, a place that you can go to get away, relax and unwind. This will help you create a stronger connection to your home or office. How can you turn a room or even a small part of a room into a haven? What does "haven" mean to you? And how can you prioritize your heart above your head once in a while?

- Feeling so inspired that you want to start your own business? Or maybe you have already dabbled in interior design, but want to focus more on the Design Psychology angle? I am always happy to encourage others to follow their hearts into an amazing career path; I honestly feel lucky to wake up every day with the opportunity to work with amazing clients, to offer advice on TV, radio and websites, and to do something that I genuinely love. While some jobs can grow dull after a short time, this field just continues to open up, evolve and inspire me on a daily basis. I love talking with people about what I do and sharing ideas! What do you want to do when it comes to design? Where do your true passions lie?

- My designer friend Lori Dennis and I developed Design Camp for adults to share top interior design trade secrets, tips and tricks to help more people perfect magazine-ready designs and places that they will absolutely love to live, work, breathe and hang out in. It is truly the ultimate "camp" experience for adults and was designed for people who are passionate about where and how they live. Design Camp is a destination for practical, applicable, real-life design insight that you won't get from traditional courses or institutions – and it is a lot of fun! The course is tailored for both design professionals and design aficionados. Are you interested in taking your passion for Design Psychology a step further? Then join us at the next Design Camp near you!

Conclusion

"Design is an opportunity to continue telling the story, not just to sum everything up."

—Tate Linden

So do you look skinny in your home?

As you have now learned, the question is really, "Do I look – and feel – great in my home or office?"

By now, I hope the answer is a resounding "yes!" and that you recognize that you can always update a room, space or your entire home if you still need to make a change. It is all about being intentional and getting inspired. When you change an environment, you can change the way you feel, behave, think and even look!

When you combine the world of interior design with the realm of psychology, you get the fascinating study of Design Psychology – the art of using function, feel and flow to make our spaces more intentional and more enjoyable and more like our true definition of "home."

The places that we live, work in and visit every day can influence everything from our attitude to our level of motivation to our overall health and wellness to our outlook on life, so creating the perfect space is incredibly important to your health and happiness. In recognition of the fact that a home or office is much more than four walls, a floor and a roof; the field of Design Psychology helps people create meaningful and fulfilling places to live, work and grow.

Why we live the way we do

Design Psychology gets to the real "why" behind the who, what, when, where and how. It is why we make certain decisions and why we live the way we do. It is also pretty fascinating, pretty powerful and pretty simple to implement in your home or your office.

I hope you have gleaned a combination of interesting background research and practical solutions to implement some Design Psychology principles and ideas in your home, your office and your life.

Regardless of where you live or your budget, you have the power to create rooms, spaces and the home and havens of your dreams, because you have the ability to live intentionally. You can remodel your entire home or simply update one corner of one room and bring this idea to life.

Whether it involves adding some new lighting, creating a new focal point in a room, clearing out the clutter that is holding you back, trying out some nature-inspired elements or new colors on the walls, or focusing on making more havens in your home, the *place you live* will affect the *way you live*, so it only makes sense to invest some time, love and energy into that place.

While checking out the latest trends is always fun, your focus should come more from what speaks to your heart, what you will enjoy for the long term, and what offers the ideal function, feeling and flow for you and your family. And it's important to recognize that you can always make a change!

When you piece the basics of Design Psychology together, you can create a "home sweet home" that not only makes you "look skinny" but – even better – makes you feel happy and fulfilled!

Resources and References

The following helpful list of resources and references will provide more information and ideas related to Design Psychology and the concepts discussed in *"Do I look skinny in this house?"*:

- My website, blog, background information, videos and more: www.kelliellis.com
- Interior Design Camp: www.designcamp.com
- Kelli Ellis How-to Videos: www.kelliellis.com/how-to-interior-design-videos/ and www.eHow.com, interior design expert.
- "House Lust: America's Obsession with Our Homes" by Daniel McGinn: www.amazon.com/books/dp/B0071UOAF8
- Theano S. Terkenli, associate professor of Human and Cultural Geography, The Cultural Landscape and The Geography of Tourism: www.geo.aegean.gr/english/people/terkenli_cv.htm

- Abraham Maslow and the Hierarchy of Needs: www.maslow.com
- Peter Walsh, amazing clutter organizer: www.peterwalshdesign.com
- Pantone: www.pantone.com
- Color Matters: www.colormatters.com
- "Color Psychology and Color Therapy" by Faber Birren: www.amazon.com/Color-Psychology-Therapy-Faber-Birren/dp/0806506539
- Spencer Institute Design Psychology Coach Certification online program: spencerinstitute.com/design-psychology-coach-certification
- HGTV: www.hgtv.com
- TLC: www.tlc.com
- The Style Network: www.stylenetwork.com
- Extreme Home Makeover: www.abc.go.com/shows/extreme-makeover-home-edition
- "Wabi-Sabi: for Artists, Designers, Poets & Philosophers" by Leonard Kohen: www.amazon.com/Wabi-Sabi-Artists-Designers-Poets-Philosophers/dp/0981484603
- "Design Psychology: Beyond Pretty Properties and Nice Knick-knacks" from Psych Central: www.psychcentral.com/blog/archives/2011/06/30/design-psychology-beyond-pretty-properties-and-nice-knickknacks
- "The Psychology of Design Explained" from Digital Arts Online: www.digitalartsonline.co.uk/features/graphic-design/psychology-of-design-explained
- E-how interior decorating tips: www.ehow.com
- Mom TV: www.momtv.com
- Blog Talk radio: www.blogtalkradio.com

Glossary

Following are helpful definitions for several terms and concepts used throughout *Do I look skinny in this house?*

Anti-Highlighting: A lighting techniques that can disguise stains or other damage by hiding them in the shadows of a room.

Biomimicry: A design method that seeks lasting solutions to human problems by imitating nature's time-tested powers and tactics. This involves taking clues from nature and then applying them to everyday life

Chromotherapy: The scientific study of color

Design Psychology: The study of design and its effects on emotions and well-being , Design Psychology is about being intentional about the function, feel and flow of your spaces.

DIY: Do it yourself (think Home Depot)

Feel: One of the design F words, feeling is simply how a space feels to everyone who uses it.

Flow: One of the design F words, flow is how movement is allowed to happen in any given space.

Function: One of the design F words, function refers to how well a space works for the people who use it.

General lighting, which is also known as **ambient lighting,** sets a mood or impression and also provides for safe circulation within a space.

Haven: A personal space of retreat, relaxation and rejuvenation

House Lust: A recent trend in the housing market where people wanted more and more and bigger and bigger when it came to their houses and living spaces.

Inspiration piece: Any item of furniture or memorabilia that provides a spark of inspiration in a room and can be made a centerpiece of design.

Sustainable design: A design principle that focuses on doing more with less, using repurposed or multipurpose pieces with an eye towards lasting and reusable design. Sometimes known as green design.

Synesthesia: A condition in which one sense triggers a response in a different sense, which is why we have physiological responses to certain colors, sights, sounds, smells and feelings.

Task lighting provides enough light to read, work or be able to safely walk through a corridor.

Trend: The recent hottest thing in design or style; trends come and go, so it's important to examine and stick with the ones that really resonate with you.

Visual interest: Lighting that adds an unexpected touch. A table that's lit from underneath or a fountain that is illuminated are two examples of lighting for visual interest.

Voice: What a room has to say to you when you listen carefully

About the Author: Kelli Ellis

"The Darling of Design and Design TV"
—Riviera Modern Luxury Magazine

Voted "Top Interior Designer in Orange County"
—OC Metro magazine

Her clients know that a home designed by Kelli Ellis is an exceptional experience, combining serenity and style. As an only child of a politician father and an uber-creative mother, Kelli began her love of media and design very early. Kelli draws continued inspiration from her travels to Europe, South America, Northern Africa and Australia, as well as her experiences living abroad. With a quick wit and down-to-earth nature, Kelli made her way into your living rooms early in her design career.

You have likely seen Kelli as the featured designer on TLCs *Clean Sweep*, two seasons of HGTV's *Takeover my Makeover*, and you watched her help fan favorites on Bravo's *Real Housewives of Orange County* transform their homes into their ultimate havens; she is also a regular on HGTV's #1 holiday hit, *Celebrity Holiday Homes,*

In addition to HGTV, TLC and Bravo, Kelli has guest appeared on NBC, CBS and ABC nationwide. The web knows Kelli from eHow. com as its resident Interior Design Expert and VandM.com Insider. You have also heard her give decor and Design Psychology advice on HGTV Radio/Sirius, MomTV and BlogTalk radio. In addition, she is also a regular keynote speaker and panelist at High Point Market and Las Vegas Market, as well as a variety of other design summits annually. Kelli was recently named as one of the Influential Women of Design at the Las Vegas Market. Additionally, she regularly contributes to HGTV.com, Riviera Modern Luxury, Star Magazine, Cosmopolitan, Redbook, Better Homes and Gardens, Vegas, TV Guide, Image, Dabble Magazine and Hearst publications nationwide. Seeing the need for her viewers to tackle their own projects, she recently created The Kelli Kit DIY design tool.

As a Certified Life Strategies Coach (CLSC) and the leading Certified Design Psychology Coach (CDPC), she has created the Certified Design Psychology Coaching program through the nationally accredited Spencer Institute online.

During her successful run on TLC's *Clean Sweep*, Kelli became a design expert in *Clean Sweep, Conquer the Clutter* book and workbook. She was also voted one of Luxe Magazine's "Editor's Top 10 Designers" and named "Top Interior Designer in Orange County" by *OC Metro* magazine. Kelli is also a featured expert in the global documentaries, "The Compass," "Riches" and "The Vow". In addition, Kelli was recently nominated for "Remarkable Woman of the Year" by the National Association of Women Business Owners (NAWBO).

Furthermore, Kelli has joined forces with award-winning designer Lori Dennis to bring Design Camp to thousands of interior designers, decorators and design lovers nationally and internationally. Join Lori and Kelli in one or more of the Design Camp locations near you: More details are now available at www.designcamp.com.

Acknowledgements

I want to first and foremost thank my family for their ongoing, unwavering love and support for all I do. My ride would be utterly impossible without them. I want to acknowledge my beautiful children Sophia and Alexa, and thank you for sharing your mother. As many working mothers understand, the push-pull of your priorities, commitments and heart-strings makes the road bumpy, at best. I hope that, through my journey, you have gleaned some respect for family, goals and hard work. You two impress me, change my mind, alter my perspective and ground me every day. I love you. Next up, my parents, Jon and Linda. As an only child of two extraordinary people, I have been blessed from day one. I have carefully watched your hard work, tenacity, drive and love for people transform your lives, but mostly the lives of those around you. You taught me to project my time, my efforts and my talents to be of service to others, and for that I am rewarded every day. My appreciation of your love and support could fill volumes, so simply,

I love you, mom and dad. To my loving husband John, you lift me up to be my best, show me there is no ceiling, no walls and no end to my creativity and dreams. Your had me at "sushi." To my extended family, marriage, blood or otherwise, thank you for your loud and written cheerleading around the globe: You're the best.

Thank you to my clients who have become friends, those of you who allow me into your lives and homes, and transform your homes into your havens. Dr. Diane Rogers, a client, a friend, a colleague and a ray of light, thank you for your words of wisdom.

Stay in Touch

I always love hearing your success stories and receiving your questions! You can find me online at www.kelliellis.com/contact-kelli-ellis.

Other great ways to connect with me include:

- My blog: www.kelliellis.com/blog
- My Facebook page: www.facebook.com/designerkelliellis
- Twitter: @designerkelli
- Pinterest: www.pinterest.com/designerkelli
- Google+: plus.google.com/111702494237571291280

Worksheets

The following eight Design Psychology-focused worksheets can help you examine your preferences, ideals and goals for your next home or office-remodeling project. Jot down your ideas, drawings and to-dos on the following pages to uncover the *why* of your likes and dislikes, your goals and your dreams.

Worksheet 1: Goal Setting and More

1. What do you love about your current home or office?

2. What would you like to change, remove or update?

3. What historical trends and styles do you particularly like? And not like?

4. Examine the people who live in your home or work in your office who are at various ages or stages in their lives. What simple updates could be made to increase their overall happiness or productivity?

Worksheet 2: Reality Calls

Pretend that you are a character on a hit TV show – it can even be your current favorite show. Walk through your own home and have a look at it from another perspective. Imagine some of your favorite characters sitting on your sofas and visiting your living room and your family room.

1. What do your spaces say about you and your character?

2. Would your home make you the main love interest, the quirky sidekick or the difficult mother-in-law?

3. Are you really creating that haven that you are looking for through TV eyes or do you need to make some changes?

4. How could your show be even more of a hit?

Worksheet 3: Home Sweet Home

1. Make up your own definition of home. What key words, phrases and ideas come up in that new definition?

2. Are there any associations with the word home that you would like to change? Or any objects you need to remove from your current home?

3. Take a look at Abraham Maslow's Hierarchy of Needs, carefully reviewing each category: Physiological, Safety, Love/belonging, Esteem and Self-actualization. Where do you fall on the chart? Are there any unmet needs you need to take care of?

Worksheet 4: The Design Psychology F words

1. FUNCTION: How do the rooms in your house or office currently function? How could they function better? Who do they need to function for?

2. FEEL: How do the rooms in your home or office feel to you and to the others who use the space? What updates could you make to make those feelings more positive?

3. FLOW: How do the rooms in your home or office flow? Are there any roadblocks that need to be removed or anything else that could be improved?

4. How do function, feel and flow come together overall in your spaces?

Worksheet 5: Lessons in Appreciation

1. When doing Lesson in Appreciation #2, take the time to write down anything that feels right about the room. What do you or did you love about it?

2. What items in the room are serving that feeling and what ones are detracting from it?

3. Now play "the company's coming game." Take a look at any room and ask yourself: What would I do in this room to update it right now if company were coming today?" How about tomorrow? In a week? In two weeks? In one month? You just gave yourself a Design Psychology to-do list that will make your next party as well as your next day with your family that much better.

Worksheet 6: Organize to Downsize

1. Make a list – or a pile – of anything you haven't seen, used or in a year. And then get rid of it!

2. What do your rooms currently say to you? Is that the message that you want to hear?

3. Assess your capacity for DIY: Do you like to do big projects, little projects or just dream up projects for someone else to work on? Be honest with yourself before tackling your next home improvement project. You can also use this space to make a list of any items you might need from the local home improvement store.

Worksheet 7: Color Me Beautiful

1. Take a tour through your house and write down the central color scheme in each room. Next to that, note any feelings about that color or colors. Which ones stand out? Which ones do you like best? And least?

2. Go through any magazines you have on hand and look for pictures or images of rooms that you really like. Notice the wall color in each picture. You should see a pattern. If so, write it down here.

3. Consider the F words along with color:
   • Function: How does this room you want to paint function? Will you use it for work, sleep or play, and what colors will inspire those activities?

   • Feel: How do you want to feel in this room? What colors will really give you this feeling and energy?

   • Flow: How does your house or office flow from room to room? Is there a unifying color that you can use on the walls, in accent pillows and pieces, and so on?

Worksheet 8: Creating Havens within Your Home

1. Draw a picture of your childhood haven or secret hiding spot (this does not need to be perfect in any way, shape or form!). If you are more of a writer, you can describe it in words (in detail) instead.

2. Ask yourself, how can I recreate this in my house today? What supplies will you need? How long do you estimate that the project will take?

Printed in the USA
CPSIA information can be obtained
at www.ICGtesting.com
JSHW022343140824
68134JS00019B/1653